HG
2463   Hoffman.
R6H6   David.

HG
2463   Hoffman.
R6H6   David.

David

David

WILLIAM HOFFMAN

Lyle Stuart, Inc. • New York

24 July 1974

Second printing; May, 1971

DAVID

Copyright © 1971 by William Hoffman

Library of Congress Catalog Card Number 76-124504

Queries regarding rights and permissions should be addressed to Lyle Stuart, 239 Park Avenue South, New York, N.Y. 10003.

Published by Lyle Stuart, Inc.
Manufactured in the United States of America

PREFACE

His grandfather was the richest man in the world.

His father built Rockefeller Center and reconstructed Williamsburg, Virginia.

One of his brothers is a four-term governor of New York.

Another of his brothers was a two-term governor of Arkansas.

His nephew expects to be president of the United States.

Yet none of these people could ever approach the power and influence he wields. His business is money. His market is the world.

He has been called a philanthropist. He has also been called an exploiter. Some people believe he is one of a troubled world's great hopes. Others believe he is one of the biggest barriers in the path of progress.

His name is David.

David

April, 1970. I called the Chase Manhattan Bank and asked to speak with David Rockefeller. The operator connected me with a secretary.

"David Rockefeller, please," I said.

"Who is calling?"

"Bill Hoffman. I'm writing a book about David Rockefeller for Lyle Stuart."

"Requests to see Mr. Rockefeller have to go through our public relations department. I can give you the number."

"Fine. I'd appreciate that."

Chapter I

*Several highly placed Republicans have pri-
vately indicated that they would be delighted to
support him* [David Rockefeller] *if he should ever
indicate an interest in the Presidency.*

New Yorker, January 9, 1965

"*I* CAN'T imagine," said David Rockefeller, when asked
about his political ambitions, "a more interesting job than
mine. . . . The bank has dealings with everything. There is no
field of activity it isn't involved in. It's a springboard for whatever interests one may have in any direction—a very good
platform from which to participate in the economic advance-
ment of the world."

On another occasion, after David Rockefeller had used a
teleprompter to deliver a lecture at Columbia University, a
member of the audience approached one of his aides.

"Isn't that the gadget President Johnson uses?" the man
asked.

"No," replied the aide, "this is the gadget David Rockefeller uses."

In the Nixon era, relative powers were discussed: "Let me

put it this way," said a prominent Delaware banker. "I don't think Richard Nixon tells David Rockefeller what to do. If anything, it's the other way around."

David Rockefeller and his aide and the Delaware banker understand what the highly placed Republicans do not: that, for David Rockefeller, the presidency of the United States would be a demotion.

David Rockefeller is, among many, many other things, the chairman of the board of Chase Manhattan Bank, probably the most powerful financial institution in the world. "He is," as *Time* magazine pointed out, "a prime mover in a profession that since the days of the Medici has heavily shaped the course of the world's economic affairs. [David] Rockefeller is one of that little group of men who sit at the financial hub of the world's wealthiest nation and by their nods give the stop or go sign to enterprises from Bonn to Bangkok."

Time magazine went on to describe what real power, not four years or eight years in the White House, but what real power is: "David Rockefeller and the Chase are expanding. . . . The Chase has 28 foreign branches of its own, but more important, it has a globe-encircling string of 50,000 correspondent banking offices."

One of the things the correspondent banking offices do is borrow money from the Chase when one of its customers needs funds to start a new business, or to expand a going one. David Rockefeller can say no to these borrowers, and thereby inhibit the growth of whole nations.

But David hardly seems the sort of person who would say no. He gives the impression of being bland and soothing, like vanilla ice cream, and he couldn't less resemble the popular image of a hard-hearted, skinflint banker clutching money to his chest in a back-room vault. Rather, David's public image is quite the opposite.

His wife admires him: "I go to all these receptions and shake hands with everybody, and haven't the faintest idea who any of them might be, but David remembers them all."

His oldest son admires him: "Dad has never tried to push me into the family businesses. He just told me to work hard, that's all, that working hard would be the greatest satisfaction of all."

His friends admire him: "There's nothing on earth I wouldn't do for David," said André Meyer, the former head of Lazard Frères. "It's not because he's a Rockefeller but because he's the kind of human being you want to do something for. I've never seen him mean. I've always seen him acting with poise and class, and greatness. In this financial jungle, you have all kinds of animals. He's the best."

His peers admire him: "David's always got an Emperor or Shah or some other damn person over here," said the late Sidney Weinberg, senior potentate of the Goldman, Sachs brokerage house, "and is always giving lunches. If I went to all the lunches he gives for people like that, I'd never get any work done."

His customers admire him: "David Rockefeller is the most important banker in New York City," said a Caracas businessman. "Therefore, he is the most important banker in the world."

Even his competitors admire him: "I can't believe that if a poll were taken today," said a downtown New York City investment banker, "to ascertain who the outstanding person in Wall Street and banking circles is, there would be anybody who could compete with David. He is the best product that the capitalist system has produced."

Perhaps. David is also an enormously wealthy man, how wealthy only he knows, he and a stable of trustees and lawyers and accountants, careful men, men who would not like the true extent of his holdings to be made public, even though those holdings have already been estimated, by various sources with various motives, at between $200,000,000 and $6,000,000,000. The top figure may be conservative.

David has more stock in the Chase Manhattan Bank than anyone else, more than $19,000,000 worth. His wife also has huge stockholdings in the bank, as do his six children and a passel of brothers, uncles, aunts, nephews, nieces, and cousins. In addition, most of the Rockefellers have large sums of money on deposit with the Chase, plus enormous amounts administered by the bank's trust departments.

The Chase is quite literally a Rockefeller bank, the family controls it, and the bank had assets, as of March 31, 1970, of $22,980,500,210. Lest anyone feel that $22,980,500,210 isn't impressive enough, the *New York Times* pointed out that "a major portion of their [Chase Manhattan's] business carried on through affiliated banks overseas is not consolidated on the balance sheet."

But total assets fail to give a true picture of the power of the Chase, much less that of David Rockefeller, who has many interests outside the bank.

The *New York Times*, July 9, 1968, reporting on a study conducted by a House Banking subcommittee headed by Representative Wright Patman of Texas, said that "A few banking institutions are in a position to exercise significant influence, and perhaps even control, over some of the largest business enterprises in the nation."

Five percent of stock in a major corporation usually assures minority control over that corporation. The Patman Report revealed that Chase Manhattan, through its combined trust departments, held 5.3% of the common stock of American National Bank & Trust of Chicago, 6.7% of Safeway Stores, 25.4% of Purity Stores, 9.5% of Arwood Corporation, 5.5% of Reynolds Metals, 6.3% of White Cross Stores, 5.1% of J. C. Penney, 5.1% of Automatic Retailers of America, 17.6% of Franklin Stores, 11% of Northwest Airlines, 6.4% of Eastern Airlines, 8.5% of Moore-McCormack, 7.8% of TWA, 6.7% of Pan American World Airways, 6.1% of Merchants Fast Motor Lines, 9.8% of Pacific Intermountain Express, 6.7% of Western Airlines, 5.6% of Penn Central, 8.8% of Consolidated Freightways, 8.9% of Roadway Express, 7.9% of Ryder System, 5.1% of Commercial Solvents, 13.5% of Universal Oil Products, 8.3% of Wyandotte Chemicals, 6.3% of Hercules, 9.6% of Air Products & Chemicals, 5.6% of Panhandle Eastern Pipeline,

5% of North Carolina Natural Gas, 5.6% of Armstrong Rubber.

Further Chase holdings were 7.8% of A. H. Robbins, 5.5% of G. D. Searle, 10.4% of Richardson-Merrell, 7.1% of George D. Roper, 11% of Varian Associates, 8.5% of Sunbeam, 8.7% of Beckman Instruments, 8.9% of Texas Instruments, 5.1% of Sperry Rand, 8.7% of Boeing, 5.3% of Crum & Forster, 7% of Diebold, 9.6% of Cummins Engine, 6.6% of Gyrodyne Company of America, 9.4% of Bausch & Lomb, 9.7% of H. H. Robertson, 5.2% of Jonathan Logan, 5.9% of CBS, 11% of International Basic Economy Corporation, 6.2% of Aircraft United, 8.5% of Addressograph-Multigraph, 7.6% of Harris Intertype, 5% of Aetna Life, 7% of American General Insurance Company, 6.7% of American Reinsurance Company, 5.2% of Allegheny Ludlum Steel, and 6.2% of National Steel.

Even a listing of the companies controlled by David's Chase Manhattan fails to give the total picture of the power of that bank, and of the one man who sits at its helm.

Through the Chase Investment Corporation, a Chase Manhattan subsidiary, the bank has a sheep- and cattle-raising operation in Australia, hotels in Puerto Rico and Liberia, a ready-mix concrete plant in Brazil, a cotton textile mill in Nigeria, a paint factory in Venezuela, a steel mill in Turkey, a petrochemical plant in Argentina, a bus line in the Virgin Islands, and bowling alleys in Great Britain.

The Chase Manhattan is like a sovereign state, except that it has more money than most. The bank even employs a full-time envoy to the United Nations, for whom the Chase serves as banker, and U Thant has been a guest at David's estate in Pocantico Hills, New York.

David wheels in international circles. He has to. The Chase Manhattan owns or controls Banco del Commerce, with 120 branches in Colombia and Panama; Banco Continental, with 42 branches in Peru; Banco Atlantida, with 24 branches in Honduras; and Nederlandsche Crediet, with 66 branches in the Netherlands. In addition, Chase Manhattan controls the Standard Bank Group, which with 1,200 branches dominates finance in Kenya, Malawi, Tanzania, Uganda, Zambia, South Africa, Rhodesia, Nigeria, Ghana, and eight other African countries.

Altogether the Chase has branches or correspondent banks in more than fifty countries around the world, has lent money in those countries, and thus has a vested interest in maintaining the established order overseas so that repayment will be guaranteed.

The Chase is booming because of the interest from these loans, but a few critics are not overjoyed by the bank's good fortune. These critics point out that the Chase Manhattan has branches in Saigon (South Vietnam), Bangkok (Thailand), Seoul (South Korea), and Athens (Greece), and that, especially in South Vietnam, where the bank has lent money to a large number of entrepreneurs, David has more than a passing interest in gaining a favorable settlement of the war.

David was well aware, however, of South Vietnam's inability to defend foreign businesses, and kept that in mind when Chase Manhattan constructed its Saigon branch. *Business Week* explained: "In the midst of a neighborhood of honky-tonk GI bars, the Saigon branches of Bank of America and Chase Manhattan Bank look like modern fortresses in granite and sandstone. . . . The banks . . . were built especially for wartime conditions—glass blocks instead of windows, and walls designed to withstand mine explosions and mortar attacks."

The *New York Times*, April 25, 1968, quotes David as saying that the Vietnam War "costs us some $1.5 billion a year in foreign exchange," but that "in the kind of world in which we live, we simply must be prepared to shoulder this kind of financial burden when necessary in the defense of freedom."

It took the Chase National Bank (the forerunner of Chase Manhattan, named in 1877 by its founder John Thompson after Abraham Lincoln's secretary of the treasury, Salmon P. Chase) until the year 1965 to go over the twelve-billion-dollar mark in assets.

Since 1965, when President Lyndon Johnson announced the

first large-scale escalation of the Vietnam War, Chase Manhattan's assets have shot up to almost twenty-three billion dollars, nearly doubling in five years what it took more than eighty years to acquire.

The use of interlocking directorates (directors on the board of Chase Manhattan Bank who also sit on the boards of other corporations) is another method of exercising control over some of America's largest businesses. Men who sit on the board of directors of Chase Manhattan also are directors (when Chase has more than one director on another company's board it will be indicated) of the following corporations: Allegheny Ludlum Steel; Youngstown Sheet and Tube; United States Steel (2); Metropolitan Life; Travelers Insurance; Jefferson Standard; U.S. Fidelity & Guaranty; Continental Insurance; Equitable Life Assurance (4); American Machine & Foundry; Bucyrus-Erie; Otis Elevator; Worthington Corporation; Veeder Industries; United Engineering & Foundry; General Foods; Lehigh Portland Cement; Chrysler Corporation; Standard Oil Company of Indiana; Stone & Webster; New York Times Company; Lily Tulip Cup Corporation; Cummins Engine; Burlington Industries; American Broadcasting Company; Standard Oil of New Jersey (2); R. J. Reynolds Tobacco; Scott Paper; International Paper; International Basic Economy Corporation; United Aircraft; Singer Company; Essex Wire; International Telephone & Telegraph; Goodyear Tire & Rubber; Arvida Corporation; Great Southwest Corporation; Grand Union; Cerro Corporation; Anaconda Copper (2); American Smelting & Refining; Titanium Metals; Chile Copper; Fansteel Metallurgical; F. W. Woolworth; Allied Stores; Federated Department Stores; R. H. Macy; Moore-McCormack; Penn Central; Detroit, Toledo & Ironton Railroad; Piedmont Aviation; Western Maryland Railway; Wabash Railroad; Commercial Solvents; Celanese Corporation; Colgate-Palmolive; General Aniline & Film; National Lead; Chemetron Corporation; Bell Telephone Company of Pennsylvania; Brooklyn Union Gas Company; Consolidated Edison of New York; American Telephone & Telegraph (2); New York Telephone Company; and Southern New England Telephone Company.

The presidency, for David, would indeed be a demotion.

David travels a lot and, naturally, is preoccupied with thoughts of money. When the bank he heads made a loan to Panamanian ranchers, he was on hand to watch cattle, which were the bank's collateral, branded with Chase Manhattan's initials. On another occasion, after a visit to Malaysia, he was asked by a vacation-planning friend what he thought of the place.

"It is surprising," replied David, "that such a small country should have such fantastic foreign-exchange rates."

Because of his travels, David is often more familiar with foreign cities than he is with American ones. His pronunciation of Teheran is flawless, yet despite speech lessons he has never been able to master Terre Haute.

Chase Manhattan's investments overseas, which are in a real sense Rockefeller investments, have been called "ours" by a long list of United States presidents, thus helping to make necessary a standing Armed Services force of more than 3,000,000 men, just in case some foreign malcontents should try to boot out the Chase, and other corporations, or, worse, try to nationalize them. David's heart pounds in dismay when he considers what might happen to his far-flung financial empire and, along with other members of his family, has tried to assure—through political appointments—that the worst never happens.

Many progressives viewed with distrust the appointment of Dean Rusk, former head of the Rockefeller Foundation, as secretary of state, but it was only one in a long series of high government positions handed to former Rockefeller underlings. The worst fears of the progressives were confirmed when Rusk eventually emerged as a fire-breathing hawk on Vietnam. Also, Rusk admitted to a senate committee that he drew severance pay from the Rockefeller Foundation while he was secretary of state.

Another of the more rabid hawks to serve as secretary of state was John Foster Dulles, also a former head of the Rockefeller Foundation. In addition, Dulles was associated with the law firm of Sullivan and Cromwell, a leading legal agent for all of the Rockefellers. It was John Foster Dulles who, as a top policy-making director for the International Nickel Company, helped arrange the agreement with I. G. Farben that permitted Nazi Germany to stockpile nickel for war purposes.

Allen Dulles, former head of the Central Intelligence Agency, was also associated with the law firm of Sullivan and Cromwell.

Eugene Black, who became head of the World Bank, was a former vice president of Chase National and now sits on the board of directors of Chase Manhattan.

C. Douglas Dillon, former secretary of the treasury, is another member of Chase Manhattan's board of directors.

John J. McCloy, former High Commissioner in West Germany, later became chairman of the board of Chase Manhattan. It was John McCloy who was instrumental in making Konrad Adenauer, his brother-in-law, chancellor of West Germany.

As mentioned, David is much more than just the driving force behind the Chase Manhattan Bank, and it seems that people in other countries are more aware of his importance than Americans are. When David visits foreign countries, the *New Yorker* reported, "the resident officials of each one naturally want to make the most of it. . . . The crowds that assemble to greet [David] Rockefeller at airports—they include not only branch-bank managers, but finance ministers, American ambassadors, reporters, photographers—are sometimes large enough to make bystanders wonder what movie star is approaching."

David rarely goes to a country without paying a call on the head of state, and these leaders usually repay the visit when they're in America. At one reception, held at his estate in Pocantico Hills, David was host to twenty-five foreign ambassadors.

"David probably knows more foreign leaders on a personal basis than the president of the United States does," said a Chase Manhattan vice president.

The *Christian Science Monitor* understated its case when it called David "a businessman who is listened to all over the world."

David often speaks for the business community as a whole. In an interview on NBC, he was asked to discuss the growing alarm in the British Parliament over the increased American ownership of English corporations. What American businessmen planned, said David, was "not less U.S. foreign investment, but more."

David visited the Soviet Union in July, 1964, and closeted himself with Russian Premier Nikita Khrushchev for two and a half hours. Later, *Pravda*'s account of the meeting accorded David the coequality he deserves: "N. S. Khrushchev and D. Rockefeller had a frank discussion of questions that are of mutual interest."

Two years after David's meeting with Khrushchev, the United States widened its trade relations with Russia, and most observers said it was a direct result of agreements reached between the two men. Even President John F. Kennedy, face to face with the Soviet premier, failed to accomplish anything of that magnitude.

But no one knew better than John Kennedy the influence David Rockefeller wields. The percentage of votes David received the *first* time he was nominated to the Harvard Board of Overseers was the highest in Harvard's history. The first time John Kennedy was nominated, and he was a United States senator at the time, he was an also-ran.

David was a not infrequent visitor to the White House during the Kennedy years. In the spring of 1962, after a dinner for André Malraux, Kennedy asked David to put his views on the national economy in a letter. David's suggestions, which consisted primarily of recommending a balanced federal budget and a lowering of corporation taxes, and Kennedy's subsequent reply, received considerable fanfare when they were reprinted in *Life* magazine.

Subsequently, corporate taxes were reduced from 52 to 50 percent in 1964, and to 48 percent in 1965.

After the Kennedy-Rockefeller exchange of letters, David was besieged by requests for money. "I have seen your opinions on the economy," said one writer. "Let me tell you about my economy: it is not very good. Please help me."

David is constantly receiving requests for loans. "It's tough enough," said an aide, "when he gets these pleas from presidents of countries, but it's worse when they're from presidents of banks."

Ferdinand Lundberg, in his 1968 best-seller, *The Rich and the Super-Rich*, discussed the international clout of the Rockefellers: "There is apparently a difference of opinion between foreign leaders (including Khrushchev and the Emperor of Japan) and the American public about the precise status of the Rockefellers. Can it be that the foreign political sharks, as they muster out the palace guard and the diplomats to greet them, are mistaken? My own view of them accords with that of the foreigners. The finpols [financial politicians] are ultra bigwigs, super-megaton bigshots, Brobdingnagian commissars of affairs. In relation to them the average one-vote citizen is a muted cipher, a noiseless nullity, an impalpable phantom, a shadow in a vacuum, a subpeasant."

James Reston, writing in the *New York Times*, November 20, 1968, compared the power of politicians to the power of big businessmen: "Western Europe is being unified, not by the political philosophers, or the Western statesmen, but by the American scientists and businessmen with their computers and their capital. That is what is worrying officials in Moscow.

"Officials here [in Russia] can deal with Dean Rusk but not with I.B.M. They are not worried about Nelson Rockefeller as a politician, but about David Rockefeller as a banker at the Chase Manhattan Bank."

David Rockefeller is six feet tall, unpretentious, placid, has a moon-shaped face with a needle nose, is slightly flabby, speaks softly, as though someone might overhear, conveys the impression of being everybody's friend, and, besides being one of the world's wealthiest and most powerful men, is, strangely, one of its most savagely disliked.

In 1963, the *Ghanaian Times*, in a bitter but revealing attack, charged: "Whilst the Governor of New York concentrates on changing the political climate in Washington to open up the trade in nuclear arms, the president of Chase Manhattan [David] is mostly concerned with commodities like copper and bananas."

The *Ghanaian Times* went on to accuse David of blocking the Organization of American States and the Alliance for Progress, of trying to overthrow the governments of Bolivia and Peru, of providing Portugal and the Union of South Africa with arms, of owning U.S. congressmen, and of using the Central Intelligence Agency and the State Department to protect his bank's widespread foreign investments.

"His contempt for the liberty and happiness of other people," concluded the *Ghanaian Times*, "doesn't embrace the whole of humanity, but only the sections falling under the scope of his bank's business, which dominates all other investors in Latin America, and is coming into South Africa, the Congo, Angola, and Southwest Africa in a big way."

Dislike of David is not confined to other countries. *Washington Star* reporter David Holmberg conducted a survey among antiwar activists, asking who was their least favorite person. The answer most given was not Richard Nixon or Spiro Agnew or John Mitchell. It was David Rockefeller, loving husband, kindly father, loyal friend, *Saturday Review*'s 1965 Businessman of the Year.

How does a man come to be so admired and so disliked at the same time? How does a man acquire so much money that his investment in a twenty-two-billion-dollar-plus bank, which is the largest individual investment in the bank, is peanuts compared to his other holdings? How does a man become so powerful that he can accomplish things that presidents can't? And what is the nature of the man whose financial arms stretch the length and breadth of the world, whose 50,000 correspondent banking offices are his envoys around the earth?

The answers lie, partly, in the incredible history of the Rockefeller family.

"A book about David Rockefeller?" the publicity man asked himself. "I'm not sure he'd like that."

"Why not?" I asked.

There was a hesitation on the other end of the line. "Any request for an interview with Mr. Rockefeller has to be screened by our office. You wouldn't mind coming here, would you?"

"Not at all."

"Tomorrow morning at eleven?"

"Fine."

"One question—if you're going to write a book about Mr. Rockefeller, won't you want to spend a lot of time with him?"

"I know he doesn't have a lot of time. Maybe I could just buy him lunch."

Chapter II

⧁⧁⧁⫸⫷⧀⧀⧀

*B*IG Bill Rockefeller was quite a character. He was born in 1810, grew to be almost six feet tall, deep-chested and muscular, agile, a powerful, confident, blustering man who believed in doing precisely what he pleased. He was flamboyant and forceful and fearless, drove fast horses and wore fine clothes, carried large sums of money without being afraid.

Big Bill Rockefeller called himself "Doctor," but he had never seen the inside of a medical school. It was a handy title, however, because he made his living selling bottled cures for cancer, or for any other ill a customer might have. Although money was scarce when Big Bill was pitching his panaceas, he was a super-huckster and always did well. He advertised himself as "Doctor William A. Rockefeller the Celebrated Cancer Specialist," and he charged twenty-five dollars a bottle for his cancer cure.

On February 26, 1837, Big Bill Rockefeller married Eliza Davison, the daughter of a prosperous farmer, and they settled in a home near Richford, New York. Eliza would give Big Bill six children: Lucy, John, William, Mary Ann, and twins, Frances (who died as a youngster) and Franklin. Eliza was red-haired, blue-eyed, slender, had little education. She was frugal, pious, deeply religious, a hymn-humming, prayer-murmuring prohibitionist who convinced her children that almost everything was sinful, except stealing. She was a sour-faced woman who preached fear and fire.

Big Bill Rockefeller was seldom at home to listen. For

months at a time he would be on the road peddling his cures, and his family's cupboard was often bare. In 1843 he was gone so long that Eliza had to borrow nearly a thousand dollars' worth of goods from the Robbins's store in Richford, a tremendous sum at the time. Later that year Big Bill moved his family to another home, in Moravia, New York, thirty miles away.

Big Bill's favorite pastime was hunting, and he was an excellent shot. Often he would give exhibitions to attract a crowd to hear his sales pitch. He would set up a manikin, place a pipe in its mouth, walk off two hundred paces, and shatter the pipe to pieces. Once he took aim at the manikin, spotted a pipe-smoking farmer, and blew the pipe out of the farmer's mouth.

Big Bill traveled as far west as the Dakotas selling his cures, and Eliza was left to raise the children, a task she undertook with an iron hand. Beatings were frequent and severe, and the offenses that merited punishment were many. Once her oldest son rescued a drowning ice skater from a creek. Eliza whipped him for being near the water.

Eliza's favorite quote was "Willful waste makes woeful want," and the saying stayed with her children their entire lives. The thing the children most remembered about their father was the delight he took in getting the best of them in business deals. He would con them out of something they considered important, then lecture them on the necessity of always being alert.

When Big Bill Rockefeller did return home, it was not always to a welcoming reception from his neighbors. In 1844 he was accused of stealing horses, and earlier an affair between him and neighbor Charlotte Hewitt had ignited a bitter feud. But in 1849 a more serious charge arose. He was accused of raping Anne Vanderbeak, a hired girl in the Rockefeller household. The case never came to trial. Big Bill avoided prosecution by moving out of the court's jurisdiction. A year later he was reunited with his family in Oswego, New York.

In Oswego Big Bill's absences became even longer, and the

raising of the children fell increasingly on Eliza's shoulders. But he was back, briefly, in 1853, to move his family to Strong-ville, Ohio, a Cleveland suburb.

Gradually Big Bill simply faded out of the picture. His visits grew farther and farther apart, and finally they ceased alto-gether. Big Bill lived to be one hundred years old, died ac-cused of bigamy, but his chief claim to fame was the fathering of his oldest son, who became the richest and most hated man in America.

John Davison Rockefeller was born July 8, 1839, near Rich-ford, New York. Very early in life John showed a healthy re-gard for money, and it is quite possible that he did indeed save the first dime he ever earned. When John was seven years old, he was raising turkeys and selling them for a profit, and keep-ing his money in a now-famous blue china bowl. Later, as his hoard grew, it required a box.

"I can still see," said John D. Rockefeller when he was an old man, "upon the mantel, the little box with the lattice that I kept my money in, silver and gold."

Soon John found other ways to make money, and he saved most of what he earned. He bought candy by the box, sold it to his brothers and sisters by the piece. At age thirteen he lent fifty dollars to a farmer at 7 percent interest.

There were many reasons why John earned, and saved: Big Bill's absences meant that the family was usually on shaky financial ground, Eliza taught that the possession of money was a sign of God's approval, and John himself, from the time he was a very little boy, always talked about doing "something big."

The story of John D. Rockefeller's rise to fortune has be-come American legend. At age sixteen he went to work for the firm of Hewitt and Tuttle as a bookkeeper, and at age eight-een he helped launch his own company, Clark & Rockefeller, at 32 River Street in Cleveland. The company dealt in farm products, which were taken on consignment and sold for a commission.

Clark & Rockefeller was successful from the first. After just twelve months the books showed a gross business of almost half a million dollars. But it was only the beginning for John D. Rockefeller, who never failed where money was concerned because he was completely devoid of emotion, totally analytical, and, once determined to go ahead, absolutely unwavering. John D. Rockefeller was also patient, thorough, unscrupulous, a man with but one overriding ambition: to become rich.

In 1859 Edwin L. Drake drilled the first American oil well, and a year later, when John was only twenty, a group of Cleveland businessmen had become so impressed with his ability that they sent him to Pennsylvania to judge whether they should invest in the new oil fields. John returned to tell them to stay out of oil producing, that the producers were cutthroat, violent men. He did say that money might be made in refining, although even that was a gamble.

John's report to the Cleveland businessmen had not been entirely truthful. The firm of Clark & Rockefeller had branched out and handled oil consignments and was aware of the huge profits in black gold. In fact, in 1863 John Rockefeller and his partner Maurice Clark joined Samuel Adams in the operation of an oil refinery, and soon the refinery was a big moneymaker. Crude oil was selling for as little as thirty-five cents a *barrel* in the fields; refined oil, which was inexpensive to produce, was bringing thirty-five cents a *gallon* in the marketplace.

In 1863 most men were fighting in the Civil War, but John had declined, later asking, "But who would have run the company?"

Who, indeed? The truth is that there would be no wars if they were left to the likes of John D. Rockefeller to fight.

In 1864 John married a girl from Massachusetts, Laura Celestia "Cetty" Spelman, whose habits, if not her looks, made her Eliza Davison's twin.

John borrowed heavily to expand the refinery ("I wore out the knees of my pants begging credit"), talked Henry Flagler, who had **access** to money, into joining the firm. John's attention to detail, his total dedication to the acquisition of money, the top men he surrounded himself with, his willingness to reinvest every penny of profit into the business, his ability to borrow large sums of money, all combined to make him the most successful refiner in Cleveland.

Those were boom times, oil was everywhere, new wells were being drilled daily, America was flourishing under a war-time economy, but John Rockefeller was not satisfied with being simply the largest refiner in Cleveland. What he wanted was to be the largest refiner in the world, the *only* refiner in the world. Later, in justifying his establishment of one of the most ruthless monopolies mankind has been forced to witness, John said simply, "Competition is a sin."

In 1865 John bought Maurice Clark's share of the refinery for $72,500 in cash. He also gave Clark his one-half interest in Clark & Rockefeller. But it wasn't until 1869 that John conceived the plan.

The plan was not a modest one. Its aim was monopoly, total, all-encompassing, worldwide.

John first went to the Lake Shore Railroad, which brought crude oil from the producing fields to Cleveland, and demanded and received a rebate of fifteen cents on every barrel shipped to his refinery. What this meant was that John paid the going rate for shipping, then was given back, under the table, a large portion of what he had been charged. For example, while competitors paid forty-two cents a barrel to ship oil from the field to the refinery, John paid only twenty-seven cents. In addition, he received another kickback when the refined oil was shipped to the marketplace.

These rebates, of course, enabled him to sell his product for a fraction of the price his competitors received, and the result was predictable: Within a year Cleveland's thirty refineries were reduced to ten. Those that had survived either had joined John or were about to go into bankruptcy.

The reason John was able to obtain huge rebates was that he was the largest refiner in Cleveland, and when a railroad balked at his demands he would threaten to ship over another line. Since he was refining fifteen hundred barrels a day in 1869, no one balked.

On January 10, 1870, John and his associates incorporated the Standard Oil Company of Ohio, and the stock issued was for one million dollars.

Had a stranger met John in 1870 and not been familiar with his business success, he probably would have considered Big Bill's oldest son a totally unremarkable person. John was quiet, handsome, dignified, a serious, earnest young man completely absorbed in the important business of getting along. John went to no plays, attended no parties, participated in no games, took part in no movements, served on no committees. In short, he minded his own business. John had joined the Erie Street Baptist Church, and it was around that organization that his leisure time was spent. He acted as usher, taught Sunday School, took up collections and was in every way the model Christian.

Yet in thinking John unremarkable the stranger could not have been more wrong, for John had a dream of conquest larger than Alexander the Great ever had, and he was utterly capable of doing whatever was necessary to make that dream a reality, regardless of who was hurt.

The next vehicle John used to carry out his plan was the South Improvement Company, which biographer Stewart Holbrook called "the boldest, the most naked attempt at dry-land piracy that had been conceived."

The South Improvement Company made contracts with the Erie, the Pennsylvania, and the New York Central Railroads that called for those lines to give rebates on all Rockefeller shipments of oil *and* on all shipments of non-Standard Oil companies. In other words, John was given a rebate each time oil was shipped by a competitor. In addition, the railroads agreed to furnish Standard with its competitors' waybills. John used the waybills to learn the prices being charged by his competition, plus the names of their customers.

Again, what John traded for these rebates was the promise to ship huge volume over the cooperating lines. It also helped, at least with the New York Central, that the son of that railroad's president happened to be a Standard Oil stockholder.

Before the South Improvement Company could be successful, the press uncovered John's plan, and the news touched off a wave of revulsion. John was hanged and burned in effigy in Titusville, Pennsylvania. A congressional investigation called the South Improvement Company "one of the most gigantic and dangerous conspiracies ever conceived." The Pennsylvania legislature rescinded the company's charter to do business.

But John, unpretentious, thoughtful, cautious, was never unprepared for contingencies. Even when his ablest competitor, John D. Archbold, began leasing refineries so he could form an organization large enough to compete with Standard Oil, John remained totally serene. Many independent refiners quickly joined Archbold, it was a way to fight the hated Rockefeller, but the ink hadn't dried on the contracts when the independents discovered they had been double-crossed. Archbold was an employee of Rockefeller, his company was a subsidiary of Standard. Later Archbold received his reward by being named president of the Standard Oil Company of New Jersey.

John D. Archbold was only one of many who threw in with John Rockefeller and emerged with enormous wealth. Present-day families that owe their fortunes to John Rockefeller's genius include the Harknesses, the Whitneys, the Paynes, the Pierces, the Flaglers, the Rogerses, the Bedfords, the Pratts, the Folgers, the Chesebroughs, and the Cutlers.

John was scrupulously honest with his partners, executives, and stockholders, but he was never accused of largess where rank-and-file workers were concerned. Like other titans of his time, he paid rock-bottom wages, especially at mines he owned in Colorado, and he consistently opposed the most elemental demands of labor. As one of his biographers, John T. Flynn, pointed out, "When Henry C. Frick shocked the country by shooting down ruthlessly the striking iron workers at Homestead, John D. Rockefeller wrote him a letter approving his course and expressing sympathy."

Despite the sleight of hand Archbold displayed in bringing independent refiners into the Standard Oil fold, the rebate was still the main weapon John employed to swallow competition. His sales pitch went like this: "Sell your refinery to me for cash. Or we'll give you Standard Oil shares for it. But if you don't join us, or sell to us, we'll crush you."

George Rice was a man who would neither sell, nor join. John Rockefeller crushed him. On one railroad Rice had to pay fifty cents a barrel to ship oil; the Standard paid twenty-five cents. On another railroad Rice paid thirty-five cents a barrel; Standard paid twenty-five cents and collected an additional ten cents on every barrel Rice shipped.

H. C. Ohlen was another whom John Rockefeller ruined. One month Ohlen shipped 29,876 barrels of oil to New York and paid $1.20 freight per barrel. Since John collected twenty cents on each of these barrels, the squeeze on one competitor in one month alone was $5,975.

In 1871 Standard Oil was the largest refining company in the world. But, as mentioned, John wanted it to be the *only* refining company, and for the next twenty-five years he poured his enormous energies into the accomplishment of that goal.

One of the methods he employed was to blow up a competitor's refinery in Buffalo, New York. For this deed John Archbold was tried and convicted and fined two hundred and fifty dollars.

Bribery was part of John's arsenal. He bought up the mayor and common council of Bayonne, New Jersey, many members of the New Jersey legislature and the Ohio legislature, and a number of important politicians in Washington. Representative Joseph Sibley of Pennsylvania, who posed as a reformer but was really a champion of Standard Oil, was on the company's payroll. While he was representing the people of Pennsylvania, Sibley also found time to be president of the Rockefeller-controlled Galena Signal Oil Company. Another congressman, John P. Elkins of Pennsylvania, accepted a $5,000 bribe from Standard Oil in 1898.

But senators are more important than members of the House of Representatives, so naturally John had a number of senators on his payroll. Senators Quay, Foraker, Penrose, Bailey, Bliss, and Scott were regular recipients of John's generosity. In 1904 alone Senator Penrose received $25,000 and Senator Bliss received $100,000 from Standard Oil.

However, there are weak links in even the strongest organizations, and Willie Winkfield, a messenger, was one. For $20,500 he sold evidence of Standard's widespread practice of bribery to William Randolph Hearst's *New York American.* Wisely recognizing that the public's memory is short, Hearst withheld the evidence until election time and then used it to drive a number of the bribe-takers out of office.

John practiced a more subtle form of bribery to assure good will from newspapers. One investigation revealed that at least one hundred and ten newspapers in Ohio alone had signed contracts to print news and editorials supplied by a Standard-supported agency in return for advertising. Standard Oil also owned, outright, large blocks of stock in a number of newspapers, including the *Buffalo People's Journal,* the *Oil City* (Pennsylvania) *Derrick,* the *Cleveland Herald,* and the *Cleveland News Leader.*

John's most publicized attempt at bribery came in 1890 when David K. Watson, Ohio's attorney general, refused a $100,000 Standard Oil bribe to stop pushing a dissolution suit against the company. Watson received his reward by being replaced.

His successor, Francis S. Monnett, turned down a $400,000 offer to quash the same lawsuit. He, too, was ushered into political oblivion when he refused.

To John's rescue came political boss Mark Hanna, a boyhood chum and later a maker of presidents. Hanna appointed an attorney general who realized that Standard Oil was being unjustly persecuted.

Some of John D. Rockefeller's apologists contend that he didn't know his company was paying off political officials. The truth is that no one knew what was going on in his business more totally than John. He was such a stickler for detail, such a believer in thrift, that he once became angry when he learned that forty drops of solder were being used to seal an oil can when thirty-nine drops would do the job.

John was also a practitioner of efficiency. He found that blotting his signature took valuable time away from other projects, so he hired a black man to stand at his shoulder with an ink blotter. It is inconceivable that John Rockefeller, who was Standard Oil's major stockholder and chief executive officer, would not have known about hundreds of thousands of dollars of company money being used to pay politicians.

John Rockefeller never blinked an eye when lying before congressional committees. In the famous Hepburn investigation he testified that he wasn't interested in gas and copper, even though Standard Oil owned a dozen corporations that dealt in those products.

When John retired in 1896—he still kept extremely close tabs on the company—at the age of fifty-seven, his Standard Oil was the largest industrial corporation in the world, "the greatest profit-generating mechanism the world has ever to this day seen."

"It made General Motors," said Ferdinand Lundberg, "even as of today look small because it included with the New Jersey Company, which alone tops General Motors in the industrial field, the present-day Indiana, California, Mobil, Marathon and many other big companies."

When John retired in 1896, Standard Oil tanks were to be seen not only at every railroad station in America, but along the Ganges, the Yangtse, and the Amazon, wherever boats or pipes or railroads or wagon wheels could transport oil. And because Standard had destroyed any semblance of competition, John could charge whatever he wished for his product. Hardly a person existed in the industrial world who did not pay the price John wanted, rather than the lower price a competitive marketplace would have dictated.

In 1896 John's wealth was estimated at $200,000,000. That would prove to be peanuts. Patents were being taken out on the automobile, and soon the oil business was changed from a kerosene to a gasoline industry, multiplying many times over the value of the Standard. By 1911 John's worth was reputed to be one billion dollars, an amount equal then to at least four times what it would be today. John was generally recognized as the richest man in the world.

For his retirement John chose an estate in Tarrytown, New York, and even though he was ringing the place with barbed wire he insisted on being called "Neighbor John."

The United States Supreme Court finally dissolved Standard Oil of New Jersey, the holding company (a corporation that owns other corporations), in 1911, but they needn't have bothered. It soon became evident that the thirty-three new corporations were all owned by the same people (John had 25 percent of the stock in each of the new companies), and that there wasn't a shred of competition among any of them.

In 1912 a new figure appeared upon the scene. His name was Ivy Lee. He was a colorful preacher, a man of God, and Stewart Holbrook wrote, "Any account of great corporations since about 1912 is inadequate without mention of Ivy Lee."

What Stewart Holbrook wrote was understatement. Without Ivy Lee American business would not be what it is today. The American people, historically slow to react to the most shocking revelations, had by 1912 reached the limit of their patience with the robber barons. Ivy Lee showed the barons how they could survive, and prosper. All that was needed was a new image, the sort Madison Avenue has become so expert at producing.

One of Ivy Lee's best-known contributions to the survival of big wealth was the shiny dime idea. He kept John Rockefeller supplied with bright new ten-cent pieces, which John readily passed out, most often when in range of a news camera. Why this scheme helped alter the public's estimation of John Rockefeller is a mystery, but it did. John was no longer a grasping materialist; he was a kindly old gentleman.

Even more decisive in the change of public opinion was the 1913 formation of the Rockefeller Foundation, which had Ivy Lee's wholehearted support and which would later be copied by a number of industrialists. How much philanthropy the Foundation has become involved in will be examined in the next chapter.

However, even if it were possible to believe that John D. Rockefeller did change from monopoly-minded acquisitor to warm-hearted giver, his ideas did not change. Commenting on the South Improvement Company in 1917, he said, "It was right. I knew it as a matter of conscience. It was right between me and my God."

John often emphasized the role God played in his success. Asked to explain the greatest fortune one man has ever accumulated, John said, "God gave me my money."

During the depths of the Depression in the 1930s, John refused to consider the situation serious. "God's in His heaven," he said. "All's right with the world."

Even as a very old man John found it difficult to resist the lure of the dishonest. He had won first prize at the Halifax (Florida) County Garden Club's annual flower show for a number of years before it was discovered he was taking credit for someone else's work.

John Rockefeller lived to be ninety-seven years old. He died in 1937 at Ormond Beach, Florida, but, unlike his wife Cetty, who had passed away twenty-three years earlier, John did not have to wait four months to be buried. Because he didn't want to be served by Cleveland tax assessors who claimed he owed millions, yet firmly believing that Cetty should be buried in Cleveland, John kept his wife's body in a New York City mausoleum until the matter could be "settled" and he could be present at the funeral without danger of losing money.

John's favorite greeting in later life was "God bless you. And God bless Standard Oil, too."

Somebody blessed Standard Oil. And the inheritors of the man who founded it. For John D. Rockefeller, Junior—"Junior" to many who knew him—life was one pleasant surprise after another.

The publicity man was short and stocky, with a bulldog face, and he wore a black suit and a bow tie. His office was spanking clean, modern; when he pressed a button I expected a mechanical hand to shoot out from his desk and light his cigarette. Instead a woman's voice came over the intercom, and he told her he didn't want to be disturbed.

"How far are you along with this book?" he asked. I could tell he didn't like the slacks and pullover sweater I was wearing.

"Two chapters," I said.

"I see."

"It would be easier to write if I could talk with David."

"Mr. Rockefeller is very busy. I'll have to check with him to find out if he'll see you."

"When will you know?"

"Perhaps in two weeks. He's out of town now."

"I'll call you then. By that time the book should be further along."

Chapter III

➤➤➤✖︎✦✦

THE man who was known as "Junior" was short, five-six, and paunchy—a shy, effeminate man who spent most of his adult life worshiping his father and gazing with amazement on the golden flow of profits that man's corporate creations made possible.

Junior was born January 29, 1874, in Cleveland, Ohio. He was John Rockefeller's fifth and last child, and only son. His first home was on Euclid Avenue in Cleveland, a street other Clevelanders dubbed "Millionaires' Row," and any resemblance between Junior's childhood and that of other young boys his age was a coincidence.

By the time he was four, Junior had three homes, the one on Euclid Avenue, a suite in New York City's plush Windsor Hotel, and a 700-acre estate in Forest Hill, a Cleveland suburb. The home in Forest Hill was the most impressive of the residences. It had a nine-hole golf course in the backyard, a lake for boating and fishing and swimming, miles of sloping countryside, expansive yards for lawn tennis, and a race track for horseback riding. Often Junior's father invited family friends to the estate, friends who were asked to pay cash for the privilege of being "guests."

Junior was surrounded by an almost all-female retinue during his growing-up years, he wasn't allowed to attend school, he had only one friend—the son of a family servant—and the first skills he acquired were knitting and sewing. The reason for this protectiveness was that his father intended to raise the perfect Baptist, a nonsmoking, nondrinking accumulator who would some day devote himself to the running of the Standard.

"It had been understood from the beginning," Junior once said, "that I was going into his office."

Junior would prove unsuited to fill his father's business shoes (more and more he would leave the operation of the family enterprises to subordinates), but he did keep his boyhood promise never to drink or smoke.

"Junior was a milksop," said a long-time family acquaintance. "He was always afraid someone was going to assault him. He wasn't a big man, you know, and he wasn't at all physical. He knew about the enemies his father had made and wasn't eager to run into any of them."

Junior was eleven years old when he moved with his family to a $600,000 home at 4 West 54th Street in Manhattan, but he was still not deemed ready to associate with other youngsters his age. Instead, private tutors came to his home, and he received additional instruction from the women who surrounded him, strict Baptists all, and from a variety of religious people who dropped in to deliver temperance lectures.

When Junior finally was allowed to rub shoulders with the outside world, nothing but the most exclusive was good enough. In 1887, at the Cutler School, his classmates included such future giants of finance as Arthur Milbank, Cornelius Bliss, Arthur Choate, James Hazin Hyde, and Cornelius Vanderbilt.

"I wasn't much of a scholar," Junior told biographer Raymond Fosdick, and his admission was probably an understatement. One class paper, written when he was at least sixteen, contained the following misspellings: "enclined," "extravigantly," "approched," "staired," "jinger."

Junior flunked the Yale entrance exam but was later accepted at Brown University in Providence, where he became a Phi Beta Kappa. Several students who had been nominated for Phi Beta Kappa refused the honor, contending that Junior's being given the award lessened its value. It may or may

not have helped that Junior's father was one of the larger con-
tributors to Brown.

Upon his graduation Junior went to work for his father at 26
Broadway, then the most famous business address in the
world. But Junior was not typical of most young men em-
barking on a career. "In my father's office," he recalled, "I
wasn't in a race with anybody. I didn't have to worry that
somebody would get my job. I was the only one and there
wasn't anybody else."

For almost a decade Junior courted Abby Aldrich, daughter
of Senator Nelson Aldrich of Rhode Island. They were finally
married but Junior, still a Mama's boy, needed reassurance
from Cetty, even eight months after the wedding had taken
place. "And now, Mother dear," he wrote, "you who saw so
clearly and even before I did what was right and best for me
to do, who helped me so sweetly and lovingly with my doubts
and uncertainties, is your judgment corroborated and do you
feel that Abby is the best wife for me imaginable? Do you
know you have never really told me what you think of her?"

Senator Nelson W. Aldrich, the father of the bride, chalked
up about as unenviable a record as any political observer
could imagine. In February, 1905, *McClure's* magazine revealed that the Rhode Island political machine, dominated by
Aldrich and General Charles R. Brayton, was thoroughly cor-
rupt, that the majority of state senators accepted bribes, that
Aldrich and Brayton and Marsden J. Perry manipulated the
senators into granting them perpetual public utility franchises,
and that Aldrich had bribed them into enacting unrepealable
laws that were worth millions to himself. Nelson W. Aldrich
was worth $50,000 when he abandoned his wholesale grocery
business to enter politics. After thirty years of public service
he was worth $12,000,000.

More than a thousand guests attended the wedding reception that followed Junior's marriage to Abby Aldrich. Wine
was served, and champagne, and a number of the teetotaling
Rockefellers were not at all pleased with Senator Aldrich's
handling of what they considered a solemn event. But cer-

tainly the bride was not upset. Abby Aldrich was attractive and talented and fun-loving; and, try as he did, her strait-laced husband was never able to bring her around to his fundamentalist thinking.

Just before the wedding took place, at least one newspaper couldn't resist the opportunity for satire.

"Common rumor has it," said the *New York Telegraph*, "that young Rockefeller's father is comfortably well off and has a nice home. It is altogether probable that the young couple will have sufficient to keep them from actual hunger even at the first."

Junior's marriage to Abby Aldrich was beneficial to the Rockefeller interests, since Senator Aldrich became Standard Oil's best friend on Capitol Hill. But it was only typical of many Rockefeller marriages, before and since, that benefited the family.

Percy Rockefeller, Junior's cousin, married Isabel Stillman, daughter of James Stillman, the president of National City Bank.

William G. Rockefeller, another cousin, married S. Elsie Stillman.

Geraldine Stillman Rockefeller married Marcellus Hartley Dodge, thus linking Standard Oil and National City Bank interests to the $50,000,000 fortune of the Remington Arms Company and the Phelps Dodge Corporation.

J. Stillman Rockefeller, a grandnephew of John, Sr., married Nancy C. S. Carnegie, grandniece of Andrew Carnegie, and their son was given the interesting name of Andrew Carnegie Rockefeller.

Edith Rockefeller, Junior's sister, married Harold F. McCormick, heir to an International Harvester Company fortune.

Edith Rockefeller McCormick's son, Fowler, a grandson of John, Sr., and Cyrus McCormick, inventor of the reaper, married Fifi Stillman, the divorced wife of National City Bank's James A. Stillman. Fifi was also the mother of Mrs. Henry P. Davison, Jr., the wife of a partner in the Morgan Bank.

Governor Nelson Aldrich Rockefeller of New York, Junior's son, was married to Mary Todhunter Clark, the granddaughter of the president of the Pennsylvania Railroad, before she divorced him so he could marry Happy Murphy.

Governor Winthrop Rockefeller of Arkansas, another of Junior's sons, married Jeanette Edris, a hotel and theater heiress.

John D. Rockefeller IV, one of Junior's grandsons, married Sharon Percy, a daughter of United States Senator Charles Percy, who himself formerly had been on the board of directors of Chase Manhattan Bank.

A list of this sort of marriages by the Rockefellers would be almost endless. Whether they were unions of convenience, like the ruling classes of Europe used to contract, or of love, is not important. The point is that an already astronomical fortune has been increased because of them. As Ferdinand Lundberg pointed out in his 1937 classic, *America's Sixty Families,* "The rich families with which the Rockefellers have interlocked in turn have been interlocked by marriages with other wealthy families, so that one can trace an almost unbroken line of biological relationships from the Rockefellers through one half of the wealthiest sixty families in the nation."

One of America's most cherished fables is that a man's rewards depend on what he contributes, how hard he works, what talents he brings to his chosen profession. Yet Junior Rockefeller, only a few years out of Brown University, found himself on the board of directors of the American Linseed Company; the United States Steel Corporation; the National City Bank; the Delaware, Lackawanna and Western Railroad; the Missouri Pacific Railroad; the Standard Oil Company of New Jersey; the Manhattan Railway Company; and the Colorado Fuel and Iron Company, to name but a few.

Except for the Colorado Fuel and Iron Company, in which Junior was the major stockholder, he must have enjoyed his youthful prestige. But what happened at Ludlow, Colorado, where the Colorado Fuel and Iron Company was headquartered, was something he couldn't have enjoyed. In fact, as far as the Rockefeller family is concerned, the tragic events at Ludlow are best forgotten.

The critical period began on September 23, 1913, when nine thousand southern Colorado miners went on strike. The miners were protesting poverty-level wages, long hours, inadequate safety precautions, and subhuman working conditions.

They were also protesting because, as Raymond B. Fosdick, one of Junior's long-time associates, was forced to point out in his otherwise totally sycophantic book, *John D. Rockefeller, Jr.: A Portrait*, "Labor conditions in the Colorado Fuel and Iron Company naturally reflected the views of its officers. Employees lived in company houses, leased to them with the agreement that cancellations could be made on three days' notice. They did their shopping at the company store. The camps themselves were 'closed camps,' generally with no public highways running through, thus giving the company the right to turn back 'undesirables,' which of course included union organizers. Posted at the entrance of each camp was usually a camp marshal, an employee of the company deputized by the sheriff and responsible for screening all incoming travelers. Company spies were employed to ferret out subversive sentiments, and although it was claimed that men were employed irrespective of their relationship to the union, it was difficult for a confessed union member to get or keep a job. Church and school activities were supervised by the company and again unsympathetic views were not countenanced for long."

Junior reacted to the plight of the miners by ignoring it. Instead he chose to listen to L. M. Bowers, the chairman of the board of directors of Colorado Fuel and Iron Company by title, but in reality a Rockefeller underling. Bowers called the union leaders "disreputable agitators, socialists and anarchists."

In a letter to Junior, Bowers wrote, "When such men as these, together with the cheap college professors and still cheaper writers in muck-raking magazines, supplemented by a lot of milk and water preachers with little or no religion and less common sense, are permitted to assault the business men who have built up the great industries and have done more to make this country what it is than all other agencies combined, it is time that vigorous measures are taken to put a stop to these vicious teachings which are being sown broadcast throughout the country."

Junior's response to Bowers' letter was to authorize the hiring of additional company guards. The guards were deputized by the sheriff, a Rockefeller employee; then they were armed. On October 17, 1913, the guards swept through the colony of miners in an armored car, riddling the tents with bullets. Several miners were killed, shot to death in their own homes, but those who survived were even more determined to win their demands.

Junior and his henchmen decided to escalate rather than negotiate. They induced the governor of Colorado to send in state militia to smash the strike. Part of the reason for the governor's action was the unfavorable press the miners had been receiving. Most newspapers had stood foursquare behind the interests of the company. The reason for this strange stand on the part of journalists was later uncovered by the United States Industrial Commission, but the findings came far too late to prevent the tragedy known as the Ludlow Massacre.

The Commission discovered that Jesse G. Northcutt, attorney for the Colorado Fuel and Iron Company, owned the *Trinidad* (Colorado) *Chronicle-News* and the *Trinidad Advertiser*. In addition, Junior owned the Pueblo *Chieftain* and was trying desperately to purchase the Denver *Rocky Mountain News*. He was unsuccessful, but like his father he knew how to turn defeat into victory. Standard Oil began to advertise in the *Rocky Mountain News*, and overnight that newspaper's editorial policy shifted to an antilabor position. Nor did the *Rocky Mountain News* want for favorable things to say about Colorado Fuel and Iron Company. The industrious Ivy Lee, operating out of New York, bombarded the paper with hundreds of false bulletins, many of which were printed verbatim.

The first action the state militia took at Ludlow was to pack the jails with hundreds of strikers and their sympathizers. Some people were held in prison for as long as six months without being charged.

The strike was seven months old when Junior was called to Washington to testify before a subcommittee of the Committee on Mines and Mining of the House of Representatives. Here's a portion of his testimony:

CHAIRMAN FOSTER: You are willing to let these killings take place rather than to go out there and see if you might do something to settle those conditions?

JUNIOR: There is just one thing, Mr. Chairman, so far as I understand it, that can be done, as things are at present, to settle this strike, and that is to unionize the camps; and our interest in labor is so profound and we believe so sincerely that that interest demands that the camps shall be open camps, that we expect to stand by the officers at any cost.

CHAIRMAN FOSTER: And you would do that rather than recognize the right of men to collective bargaining? Is that what I understand?

JUNIOR: No, sir, rather than allow outside people to come in and interfere with employees who are thoroughly satisfied with their labor conditions.

The miners were so satisfied with their labor conditions that they were still on strike April 20, 1914, when thirty-five militiamen, stationed on a hill overlooking the colony of miners and their families, armed with machine guns that had been stored in the office of the *Trinidad Chronicle-News,* let fire a murderous volley of bullets. Several miners were shot to death, more than a dozen others were wounded, but the militia weren't satisfied. Their intent was to break the spirit of the strikers once and for all. They stormed the tent colony and burned it to the ground. Two women and eleven children, trying to escape the conflagration, suffocated to death at the bottom of a cave.

The nation was outraged. The name of Rockefeller was denounced from one end of the country to the other. Outraged workers in Colorado looted buildings and burned mines. Workers in other states stayed off their jobs to express sympathy. Even the newspapers, traditionally antiunion, scored the officers of Colorado Fuel and Iron Company, and especially Junior.

But for all intents and purposes Junior had won. Altogether, twenty-seven people had been killed, and the miners wanted no more violence. On April 29, 1914, Martin Foster, chairman of the subcommittee before which Junior had appeared, sent the younger Rockefeller the following telegram:

"William Green, Secretary-Treasurer of the International Mine Workers' Union, makes public statement that mine workers will waive any recognition of the union or unionizing camps. Are you willing to enter into negotiations for settlement of strike on that basis and stop killing of men, women, and children? I strongly urge you to do so, and believe that the strike can be ended without recognition of the union and all the other differences can be amicably settled. In my judgment it is your duty to do so."

Junior was unmoved by Martin Foster's plea. He wanted total victory. Here's the conclusion of his reply to Foster's telegram:

"We cannot enter into negotiations of any character with the officers and agents of the United Mine Workers of America, who alone are responsible for the terrible reign of disorder and bloodshed, which has disgraced this State. Instead of it being our duty to do so, we conceive it to be the duty of the U.M.W. of A., who called the strike, to now call it off. They can do so if they see fit, and by so doing they will, within an hour, in a great measure restore industrial peace and prosperity in this State."

When Junior's reply was made public, he was accorded an honor his father had known earlier: He was burned and hanged in effigy. Mass meetings were held, there were public parades through the streets of Manhattan, demonstrators picketed the Rockefeller office at 26 Broadway, the house on 54th Street, and the estate in Tarrytown.

But Junior refused to budge. Perhaps it is understandable. He had never had to go into the bowels of a mine to earn a living, indeed he had never had to earn a living at all, so it would have been difficult for him to relate to the problems of those less fortunate than himself.

Fifteen months after it had begun, in December, 1914, the miners voted to end the strike. They had not won a single demand.

The Rockefeller image was scarred by the events at Ludlow and, with the urging of Ivy Lee, Junior set about restoring it by giving away huge sums of money. The tactic eventually worked, just as it had for his father. It worked so successfully, in fact, that decades later two of Junior's sons became state governors, and one of these came within an eyelash of the presidency.

Most people consider John D. Rockefeller and his heirs to be philanthropists, benefactors of mankind. This notion has been fed constantly by the Rockefeller publicity bureaus, the successors of Ivy Lee. But is it true? Have the Rockefellers really given away more than a billion dollars? Is it possible that men whose entire lives were dedicated to accumulating money were also dedicated to giving it away? A close look at some of the more ballyhooed Rockefeller gifts perhaps will provide an answer.

In 1889, when John, Sr., made his first donation to the University of Chicago, criticism of the Standard Oil monopoly, especially in the Middle West, was threatening to become disastrous.

In 1902, with President Theodore Roosevelt publicly lambasting Standard Oil, John, Sr., announced the formation of the General Education Board, which he capitalized at $1,000,000.

In 1905, with Roosevelt even more vocal and enjoying his

reputation as a "trustbuster," John, Sr., turned over an additional $10,000,000 to the General Education Board.

In 1907, with Congress threatening to pass an inheritance tax law and with Judge Kenesaw Landis only days away from ruling on an important railroad rebate case (he fined Standard Oil $29,000,000, but the fine was later thrown out), John, Sr., announced that "for the benefit of mankind" he was giving an additional $32,000,000 to the G.E.B.

In 1910, several days before Standard Oil attorneys filed briefs in a crucial antitrust suit pending in the United States Supreme Court, John, Sr., gave $10,000,000 to the University of Chicago.

In 1913, only two and a half months before the Sixteenth Amendment (Income Tax) became law, John, Sr., gave the Rockefeller Foundation $10,000,000.

In 1917, 1918, and 1919, when income tax rates had become almost punitive because of the war, Junior and his father gave more than $200,000,000 to the General Education Board, the Rockefeller Foundation, and the Laura Spelman Rockefeller Memorial. It should be pointed out that the Rockefellers, who were very eager for the United States to enter World War I, made far more than $200,000,000 from that conflict.

Between 1920 and 1932, Junior was the principal Rockefeller philanthropist. John, Sr., was too busy finding ways to transfer his fortune to his heirs (when he died he had gotten rid of everything but $26,410,837) without their having to pay inheritance taxes, to be much interested in charity. Junior, however, who was farther away from the grave, had discovered that under Internal Revenue Service laws it was more profitable to give away 15 percent of his income than it was to retain it and pay taxes on everything he earned.

In 1936, nine days after Franklin Roosevelt had asked Congress for higher taxes, Junior "gave away," according to his publicists, 2,100,000 shares of Socony Vacuum. Since the recipient of this generosity was not revealed, it was widely believed that he had given the shares to his children.

In 1960, when Junior died, it was announced that his will had provided for a $75,000,000 gift to the Rockefeller Brothers Fund, a foundation. However, before dying, he had divested (given to his children to avoid taxes) himself of all but $150,000,000, half of which was given to the foundation and half to his wife.

But the $75,000,000 "given" to the Rockefeller Brothers Fund was not a gift at all. Under the inheritance tax law as revised in 1948, over Harry Truman's veto, half of any estate, if it goes to a spouse, is nontaxable. Since the $75,000,000 given to his wife was nontaxable, and since the $75,000,000 given to the foundation was nontaxable, Junior niftily avoided paying cent-one in taxes on an estate of $150,000,000.

In 1970, with Nelson Rockefeller running for a fourth term as governor of New York State, it was announced that Nelson was giving $1,500,000 worth of land for a state park.

It is clear, as Ferdinand Lundberg pointed out in *The Rich and the Super-Rich*, that "the foundation has benefited its sponsors more than it benefited the world."

Nevertheless, those who toil in the Rockefeller publicity mills deserve some sort of notice for possessing a certain *chutzpah*. The gifts they credit their employers with having given include a $250,000 donation to the American Petroleum Institute, an outfit whose main function is lobbying for protective tariffs; a $510,042 donation to the Republican National Committee, a group that certainly has been philanthropic to the Rockefellers through the years; and a donation to the Anti-Saloon League.

Also included in the more than one billion dollars the publicists claim their bosses have given is interest on moneys originally donated. Thus, when John, Sr., gave $10,000,000 to a foundation, and that foundation, through shrewd investment, turned the total into $20,000,000, the higher figure was listed as his gift in future publicity blurbs.

In most cases where the Rockefellers have donated money, they have insisted on maintaining *control* of that money. In 1929, when Junior wanted to oust Robert Stewart from the board chairmanship of the Standard Oil Company of Indiana, he was able to vote not only his own shareholdings but also those of the Rockefeller Foundation and the General Education Board. In addition, maintaining control of the "donated" funds means that the money can be used to purchase expensive paintings for the donor's home, that the money can be used to pay the salary of relatives and friends and potential political allies, that the money can be lent at cut rates to large corporations, that the money can be used to research new products that will be salable on the open market, etc.

Ferdinand Lundberg, pointing out the paradox of giving, declared: "The rich grow richer and more powerful by the practice of philanthropy."

Abby Aldrich Rockefeller died in 1948 and Junior remarried in 1951, at the age of seventy-seven. His bride was Martha Baird Allen, the wealthy widow of Arthur Allen, a former classmate of Junior's at Brown University.

Following in his father's footsteps, Junior maintained unusual notions about the family's money. "We are merely the stewards of the Rockefeller fortune," he said in 1955. "Its real proprietor is God."

Thanks to the wealth his father gave him, Junior lived the good life. He traveled extensively, lived amidst sultanlike surroundings, collected paintings and sculptures and tapestries, wheeled in the highest echelons of corporate finance, amused himself with projects like the building of Rockefeller Center and the restoration of Williamsburg, Virginia; but, most important, when he died at the age of eighty-six in 1960, he had already passed on to his children—Abby, John III, Nelson, Laurance, Winthrop, and David—more money than his father had given him.

April turned to May. I called David's publicity man.

"Bill Hoffman here. You know, the fellow who's writing the book."

"Yes. Mr. Hoffman. How are you?"

"I'm fine."

"Mr. Hoffman, I spoke with Mr. Rockefeller about your book. We're wondering exactly what kind of approach you're taking."

"A truthful one."

"Could I take a look at what you've done? I think you said you had two chapters finished."

"Three are finished. And I shouldn't think you'd want to take a look at them. People might get the impression it's a house biography."

"I see."

"What about David? I'd like to meet him."

"He was very interested in your project, but he thought I should look at it first. However, let me talk to him again. Unfortunately. . . ."

"He's out of town."

"Right. But give me a call in a couple weeks."

"Fine. In the meantime I'll just keep writing."

Chapter IV

->>><<<-

*T*HE oldest of Junior's five sons, John D. Rockefeller III, was born in New York City on March 21, 1906, and attended the Browning School in Manhattan and the Loomis School in Connecticut before obtaining a B.S. from Princeton. John III is the least colorful and least accomplished of the Rockefeller brothers. He was more than forty years old before, as Winthrop Rockefeller said, "he wanted to do something completely on his own."

John III is reticent, cautious, shy, a man who, like Junior, would have seemed an extremely unlikely candidate for success had his name not been Rockefeller. But that is his name, and biographer Joe Alex Morris was able to list thirty-six boards and committees of which he had been a member.

Like all Junior's sons, except Winthrop, John III spent World War II far removed from the action. He was commissioned a lieutenant commander in the United States Naval Reserve and observed the progress of the conflict from Washington, D.C.

John III is, or has been, chairman of the Rockefeller Foundation; chairman of the General Education Board; chairman of the national council of the United Negro College Fund; chairman of the Lincoln Center of Performing Arts; chairman of the Population Council, Inc.; chairman of Products Asia, Inc.; chairman of Products India, Inc.; president of the Japan Society, Inc.; president of the Asia Society, Inc.; president of the Agricultural Development Council; a director of Rockefeller Center; and a trustee of Princeton University and the Harvard-Yenching Institute.

John III has also been a special assistant to the undersecretary of the Navy, a consultant of the Dulles Mission to Japan on the peace settlement in 1951, and a U.S. delegate to the Japanese peace treaty conference in San Francisco, also held in 1951.

A man who could attain all these exalted positions might be hailed as superhuman, at least by those who do not understand the honors and adulation showered on people who have done nothing more than inherit great wealth. Even nations have seen fit to honor John III. He has been given such blood-stirring awards as the Order of Auspicious Star of China, the Order of the British Empire, the Grand Cordon of the Star of Ethiopia, the Most Exalted Order of the White Elephant of Thailand, and the Ordre des Millions d'Elephants et du Parasol Blanc of Laos.

Especially in view of the awards from Laos and Thailand, and the fact that the Rockefeller brothers have investments in those countries, it is easy to understand John III's occasional hawkish remarks on Vietnam.

Perhaps John III's Number One contribution to the nation will prove to be the siring of John IV, who, according to the December 7, 1968, issue of the *New Republic*, "has absolutely no doubts about being elected governor of West Virginia four years from now. The only question is if he will run for that, or for the United States Senate."

Nelson Aldrich Rockefeller, Junior's second-oldest son, was born on John, Sr.'s sixty-ninth birthday, July 8, 1908, and Nelson attended Manhattan's Lincoln School at 646 Park Avenue. He couldn't get into Princeton because of grades, so he had to settle for Dartmouth where, along with Walter Chrysler, he decided to earn some pocket money by putting out a magazine. The venture failed, however, because the magazine was so expensive no one could afford it.

In 1930 Nelson married Mary Todhunter Clark, a Philadelphia socialite and the granddaughter of the president of the Pennsylvania Railroad. Their honeymoon consisted of a one-year around-the-world trip which included visits with heads of state, Standard Oil executives, and other industrial leaders associated with Rockefeller enterprises.

Back from the honeymoon, Nelson began to lease office space in the then being constructed Rockefeller Center. This was the Depression, money was short, but Nelson was not to be stopped. He leased five million square feet of office space in Rockefeller Center by buying up the leases of clients who were in other buildings. Soon, however, he found himself faced with a charge of unfair leasing practices and a $10,000,000 damage suit filed by August Heckscher, a builder and philanthropist. The lawsuit was later dropped, or settled out of court, before it came to trial.

Nelson made other youthful blunders. He commissioned Diego Rivera, then the finest muralist in the world, to paint what was to be the chief mural in Rockefeller Center. Given a free hand, Rivera painted a heroic head of Lenin, and a girl with venereal disease who was supposed to symbolize life under capitalism. The mural had cost $21,500, but Nelson ordered it destroyed.

Nelson also passed up World War II, heading instead an agency called the Office of the Coordinator of Inter-American Affairs. Later Franklin Roosevelt made him an assistant secretary of state for American Republics Affairs, and it was in this position that he was instrumental in getting Argentina, headed by Juan Perón, admitted into the United Nations.

Nelson quit his job as assistant secretary of state in 1945 when it became clear that the United States wasn't interested in putting as much prestige and money behind Latin American development schemes as Nelson thought they deserved. Nelson's interests south of the border were already obvious. He had large stockholdings in Creole Petroleum in Venezuela and had established an enormous ranch near Valencia. The ranch was five times larger than the combined boroughs of New York City.

Although Nelson's marriage wasn't officially terminated until 1962, it was probably on the rocks as early as 1948. According to biographer William Rodgers, stories of Nelson's romantic adventures, especially in Venezuela, were liberally discussed in the quiet offices of 30 Rockefeller Plaza. Nelson had five children at the time—Ann, Steven, Rodman, and the twins, Michael and Mary—but his enormous wealth and rugged good looks made him a ready target for the fairer sex. Rodgers told of one young woman with whom Nelson was associated, a stunning girl who eventually married, and whose husband was packed off to Latin America on a well-paid assignment while she remained in New York on Nelson's personal staff.

In 1952 Nelson joined the Eisenhower Administration as chairman of the President's Advisory Committee on Government Organization. It was never clear exactly what Nelson's duties were, though he did attend meetings of the National Security Council and the Cabinet and helped Eisenhower formulate the "Open Skies" nuclear arms proposal.

In 1958, wearing a beanie and swinging in a hula hoop, Nelson ran for the governorship of New York against Averell Harriman, himself a multimillionaire. Nelson charged that taxes were too high under Harriman, but as soon as he was elected he had new taxes enacted which compelled 300,000 low-income families to ante-up, where previously they had been exempt.

Nelson was by far the richest American ever to be elected to high public office. "Only in the United States," said a puzzled head of state when he visited Nelson in 1959, "would the people be asked to choose between a billionaire and a multimillionaire."

Nelson misunderstood what his visitor meant. "Yes," he replied, "it's a great country. It could only happen here."

At the time of his election Nelson was chairman of three corporations, on the board of eighteen others, and headed an advisory commission on the reorganization of the federal government.

Nelson's first term as governor was devoted primarily toward two ends: getting himself elected president and urging people to build bomb shelters. At first he wanted to make the bomb shelters mandatory, but the idea was subjected to such ridicule that he backed down. Still, Nelson intended to be safe. At a cost to the taxpayers of $8,000,000 he had a shelter constructed near the capitol building in Albany.

Nelson was reelected in 1962, again promising no increase in taxes. Before this term was up, however, he had enacted a 5 percent sales tax, a levy which clearly penalized the poor more than the wealthy. He also voted against a raise in the New York State Minimum Wage, almost at the same time boasting that he hadn't raised corporate taxes a penny and that he had no intention of doing so.

Mary Todhunter Clark obtained a Nevada divorce in March of 1962, and on April 1, 1963, Margaretta Murphy received an Idaho divorce from her husband James, a microbiologist for the Rockefeller Institute. "Happy" Murphy gave up custody of her four children and on May 4, 1963, became Mrs. Nelson Rockefeller. The newlyweds took a three-week honeymoon at the Venezuela ranch, then went to the Virgin Islands to a hotel the Rockefeller brothers own.

Happy had signed away her children to marry Nelson, but soon she had a change of heart. She kept her four-year-old daughter at the executive mansion and initiated a lawsuit for the custody of all the children. The *New York Daily News* reported that a clergyman, the Reverend Harald E. Bredesen, had joined with many others in expressing sympathy for Dr. Murphy, "who, having seen his first wife leave him, is now threatened with deprivation of his children. . . . Having left him [Mrs. Rockefeller] now seeks to take her children with her, thus making his desolation complete. What was his offense? Simply that another man, whose power and prestige were as great as his principle is small, coveted his wife and she coveted him. . . . To have him she was willing to break up her marriage and sign away her children. Now that she has him she wants her children, too. Her desire is quite natural and quite unjust."

Political pundit Gore Vidal, saying that Nelson's private business was his own, went on to say: "Anyone who could so misjudge the temper and prejudices of the American middle-class, and flout them so dramatically, is probably unfit for the office of the presidency."

Happy lost her custody suit and was ordered to return her four-year-old daughter to Dr. Murphy. And Nelson lost his bid for the 1964 Republican presidential nomination to Barry Goldwater.

Although Nelson was eager for people to pay the sales tax, he himself found a way to avoid it. He and his brothers founded the Greenrock Corporation, a tax dodge. Biographer William Rodgers explained:

"Under the sales tax law, the levy is collected from the ultimate consumer. Corporations which purchase goods for resale do not, of course, pay the tax, nor do certain exempt enterprises, such as a farm, pay sales tax on equipment or supplies needed to operate the place. When Greenrock makes purchases required in the management and operation of the Rockefeller estate, sales tax exemption can be claimed under control No. 13-1929826, which is the control number assigned by the State Department of Taxation and Finance to the company owned by Nelson and his brothers."

Also, as Rodgers pointed out in his excellent book, *Rockefeller's Follies,* Nelson has consistently sided with the interests of the Consolidated Edison Company, New York's worst polluter, and against the interests of average citizens. But Nelson's position is understandable. The Rockefeller Foundation has held shares in Con Ed in amounts up to $2,600,000, and Junior's children all have large shareholdings in the company, lumped together, probably the controlling shareholdings.

Fortunately, on the issue of Con Ed the populace seems to know where Nelson stands. On April 22, 1970, "Earth Day," Nelson tried to deliver a speech extolling the desirability of clean air and fresh water. So lusty were the boos and catcalls that he was forced to give up the effort.

In 1965 Nelson rammed through the legislature a bill calling for more than $250,000,000 of public money to build an expressway which would run adjacent to the Rockefeller holdings in Pocantico Hills.

"The fact that the new superhighway would dislocate Rockefeller neighbors," wrote biographer Rodgers, "who cherish their homes in this beautiful section of Westchester, doesn't seem to bother the Governor at all. Nor is he troubled with the cost of building this superhighway, for which there is clearly no present need and will not be until such time that Rockefeller or his heirs decide to develop the northern parts of their huge property."

In other words, Nelson's expressway, to be constructed by more than $250,000,000 of the public's money, will benefit only the private interests of the Rockefellers.

In 1966 Nelson was reelected for a third term as governor, and he continued to show that his true interests were with the business community, and not with the average taxpayer.

In 1965 a total of 25 percent of New York State's revenue came from taxes on business profits. In 1968 only 16 percent of revenue came from taxes on business profits. In 1970 the figure was down to 14 percent. In addition, New York has no progressive personal income tax above $23,000 a year.

In 1969 Nelson made a fact-finding tour of Latin America for President Richard M. Nixon. Here is what happened:

In Honduras there was widespread rioting, and one student was killed.

In the Dominican Republic a Standard Oil refinery was blown up.

In Costa Rica two thousand students demonstrated.

In Panama the National Guard had to be called out.

In Venezuela the government had to cancel Nelson's visit. Students had seized university buildings, and there was street fighting with rocks and pistols.

In Colombia a 20,000-man special security force was called out to try to control student strikes and heavy street fighting.

In Ecuador Nelson's car was almost overturned. Ten demonstrators were killed by police.

In Bolivia Nelson's scheduled twenty-two-hour visit was cut to three hours in the airport because of rioting.

In Paraguay Nelson was embraced by the dictator Alfredo Stroessner while demonstrators burned an American flag.

In Chile Nelson wasn't allowed into the country. Nationwide strikes and demonstrations had forced the cancellation of his visit.

In Brazil Nelson's stay was relatively calm. The government had arrested thousands of potential demonstrators, and press censorship had eliminated anti-Rockefeller articles.

In Uruguay the General Motors plant was burned down.

In Argentina nine Rockefeller-owned supermarkets were bombed and burned. There was also a nationwide labor strike, and one demonstrator was killed by police.

President Nixon has not suggested any more Latin American fact-finding tours for Nelson.

Nelson Rockefeller has been an outspoken champion of the Vietnam War, has come out in favor of right-wing military juntas in Latin America to "stabilize" the economic climate, has supported the deployment of the ABM system, has backed Richard Nixon's veto of the 1970 education appropriation bill, and was chiefly responsible, in 1969, for trimming welfare payments to already impoverished New York residents.

Nevertheless, he was reelected for a fourth term as governor in 1970, defeating Arthur Goldberg. Like his brothers, Nelson does not lack for awards. He holds the Order of Merit of Chile, the National Order of the Southern Cross of Brazil, and the Order of the Aztec Eagle of Mexico.

Laurance Spelman Rockefeller, born May 26, 1910, the third of Junior's sons, attended the Lincoln School (as did all the brothers except John III), and later received a B.A. in Philosophy from Princeton. One of the least fearless predictions ever made was when his class voted him "most likely to succeed."

Of the five brothers, Laurance is the wheeler-dealer. He styles himself a "venture capitalist," but a more accurate term might be "war profiteer." The March, 1955, issue of *Fortune* magazine listed such stockholdings as Reaction Motors, which makes rocket engines (21%); Marquardt Aircraft, ramjets (20%); Wallace Aviation, jet engine blades (27%); Flight Refueling, aircraft refueling (30%); Airborne Instruments Laboratory, electronic research (24%); New York Airways (3%); Piasecki Helicopter (17%); and Nuclear Development Associates (17%).

In addition, Laurance bought into North American Aviation, along with Eddie Rickenbacker, and the company was later converted into Eastern Airlines. He also bought into the then limping J. S. McDonnell Aircraft Corporation, which is now McDonnell-Douglas, one of the nation's ten largest defense contractors.

Laurance spent World War II in Washington, D.C., with the Navy's Bureau of Aeronautics. Actually, Laurance was a liaison officer between the Navy and aircraft production plants! He left the service with the rank of lieutenant commander.

Just as World War II had been good to Laurance Rockefeller, so too was the Korean War. The J. S. McDonnell Aircraft Corporation produced the Phantom and Banshee jet fighters which enabled the United States to control the air in Korea.

Laurance also made huge profits from his investments in Piasecki Helicopter. Just two months before the United States entered the Korean War, Laurance had been advised to close up shop, that there was no market for helicopters. Because of war contracts, however, Piasecki's stock skyrocketed from two dollars a share to thirty dollars a share (adjusted for split) in only four years.

Another company that benefited from the Korean War was Reaction Motors. Stock in that outfit soared from four dollars to twenty-three dollars (adjusted for split) in three years.

The secret, said Laurance, was in "putting the companies' best foot forward with the government."

Laurance was being modest. The methods needed to reap huge profits from defense contracts are much more complicated than he explained. Here's the way a well-known author/economist put it: "The most successful publicized operators in munitions stocks have been the Rockefeller brothers, with their promotions of McDonnell Aircraft, Thiokol Corp., Itek Corp., and many others. With investments in the tens and hundreds of thousands, aided by their government contacts they have repeatedly profited to the extent of millions and tens of millions. Their technique is repeated over and over: they put a small amount in a company; get it munitions business; have its stock sold to the public at ten to a hundred times the original cost; sell what they want, subject to only a 25% capital gains tax, and keep enough stock to retain control, if they wish."

It also helped when Laurance or the other brothers invested in shaky operations that they could call on the skills of people already employed by the Rockefeller empire, not to mention the fact that brother David and the Chase Manhattan Bank could be counted on to provide easy credit terms.

Fortune magazine reported that four out of five of Laurance's ventures were successful.

Of all the brothers, Laurance most resembles his grandfather. He has a sardonic humor, is calm, sophisticated, urbane. He flies his own plane and often comes to work in Manhattan via a cabin cruiser that has a PT-boat hull. He married Mary French on August 15, 1934, and she bore four children —Laura Spelman, Marion French, Lucy Aldrich, and Laurance, Jr.

In 1958 Laurance was on a panel which issued a policy report, drafted by Henry Kissinger, entitled *International Security—The Military Aspect*. The panel recommended successive additions in government defense spending of $3,000,000,000 each year until 1965. Incidentally, President

Kennedy increased defense spending even more than Laurance's panel had recommended.

Laurance Rockefeller's name has often been linked with conservation. In 1958 Dwight Eisenhower appointed him chairman of the Outdoor Recreation Resources Review Commission, established by Congress to make recommendations on the country's recreational resources. Laurance purchased the Danderberg Mountain on the Hudson River and gave it to the Palisades Interstate Park. He also gave land in the Virgin Islands to the U.S. National Park Service.

However, Laurance has not always been the perfect conservationist. He has not seen fit to sell his large shareholdings in the Consolidated Edison Company, nor has he been heard raising his voice against the assault Con Ed is making on the environment. In fact, Laurance has been known to profit where conservation is concerned. In 1966 a committee he headed accepted $270,000 of taxpayers' money from Nelson Rockefeller to make studies of a proposed project to save part of the Hudson River.

Even for a Rockefeller, Laurance seems unusually active. He is, or has been, chairman of Rockefeller Brothers, Inc.; chairman of Caneel Bay Plantation, Inc.; chairman of Rockefeller Center, Inc.; chairman of the Memorial Sloan-Kettering Cancer Society; chairman of the New York State Council of Parks; a director of Filatures et Tissages Africains; a director of International Nickel Company of Canada; a director of Olin Mathieson Chemical Corporation; a director of the Cape of Good Hope Corporation; a director of the Dorado Beach Hotel Corporation; a director of the American Committee of International Wildlife Protection; a director of Resources of the Future; a director of the American Planning and Civic Association; a director of the Hudson River Conservation Society; a member of the Corporation of Massachusetts Institute of Technology; a director and trustee of the Rockefeller Brothers Fund; a trustee of the Conservation Society; a trustee of the YWCA; a trustee and president of Jackson Hole

Preserve, Inc.; a trustee of the Alfred P. Sloan Foundation; a trustee and vice president of Sealantic Fund; a trustee and president of the American Conservation Association; a trustee and vice president of the New York Zoological Society; and a commissioner and vice president of the Palisades Interstate Park Commission.

It is assumed that he has done justice to all these positions.

Laurance holds memberships in the most exclusive clubs. Among these are the River, Princeton University, Downtown Association, Brook, Seawanhaka, Sleepy Hollow, and Knickerbocker.

"At the Metropolitan or the Union League or the University," Cleveland Amory quoted a clubman, "you might do a $10,000 deal, but you'd use the Knickerbocker or the Union or the Racquet for $100,000 and then, for $1,000,000 you move on to the Brook or the Links."

Laurance doesn't belong to the Links, but brothers Winthrop and David do.

Laurance possesses awards lesser mortals seldom hear of. He is a Commandeur de L'Ordre Royal du Lion of Belgium, a recipient of the Conservation Service award of the U.S. Department of Agriculture and of the Horace Narder Albright Scenic Preservation medal.

Winthrop Rockefeller, Junior's fourth son, was born on May 1, 1912, and attended the Lincoln School of Columbia University Teacher's College and the Loomis School in Windsor, Connecticut. He entered Yale in 1931 but dropped out, rather than flunk out, in 1934.

Winthrop is the most independent of the five brothers. He is active, outgoing, friendly, a big—six-three, two hundred and fifty pounds—blustery man who seems to have followed his own lights rather than those set out for him by his father.

After leaving Yale, Winthrop went to the Texas oil fields to work as a common laborer. So hated were his father and his grandfather that Winthrop needed constant protection by bodyguards. When he returned to New York City in 1936 to study finance at the Chase National Bank, he obtained a permit to carry a gun as protection against "fanatics." In 1938 Winthrop went into the foreign department of Socony Vacuum.

Winthrop is the only son of Junior Rockefeller to see combat during World War II. It is to his credit that he did, because his family connections certainly could have kept him out of the action. Winthrop joined the Army as a private, came out as a lieutenant colonel. He was with the 77th Infantry in the invasions of Guam, Leyte, and Okinawa, and he was seriously burned when a kamikaze fireballed into the troopship *Henrico*. Winthrop was awarded the Bronze Star with oak leaf cluster and the Purple Heart.

Winthrop is the most militant of the brothers in advocating a stepped-up war in Vietnam.

In 1946 Winthrop went back to work for Socony Vacuum, but he spent more time in New York nightclubs than he did in the office, and soon the newspapers were gleefully chronicling his high living, and speculating whether he would wed Mary Martin. Winthrop no longer makes the front pages with his night life, but he is still an extremely heavy drinker.

Tom Murton, writing in *Accomplices to the Crime*, an exposé of the Arkansas prison system, gave his first impressions of Winthrop: "He had a disarming smile with imperfect teeth mottled by the two packs of unfiltered Picayune cigarettes he smokes a day. His only distracting trait was a nervous tic which caused his head to bob and weave for a few moments just before he started any statement. His ruddy complexion, which I then took as a sign of health and body tone, I realized later was probably the result of excessive drinking habits."

Winthrop married Mrs. Barbara "Bobo" Sears, formerly Jievute Paulekiute from the Pennsylvania coal country, at fourteen minutes past midnight on Valentine Day, 1948, and a son, Winthrop Paul, was born the following September. The marriage was a disaster from the start. Bobo was too ebullient for the family's conservative tastes (and even Winthrop's, for that matter), and soon they were separated.

"Gossip columnists," wrote *Time* magazine, "who had promoted the union as a real-life sequel to Cinderella and Prince Charming, billed it subsequently as Beauty and the Beast, casting Win as the brutish, skinflint millionaire."

The divorce became official on August 3, 1954, and Bobo received a $6,393,000 settlement, plus custody of the child. According to *Time,* Winthrop "reaped a press worse than any Rockefeller since John D., Sr. incurred the muckrakers' wrath half a century before."

Matters hadn't been improved any by the insinuation brought out during the lawsuit that Winthrop owned a pornography collection valued at more than one million dollars.

In 1954 Winthrop moved to Morrilton, Arkansas, where he had purchased nine hundred acres of land on Petit Jean Mountain, sixty-five miles northwest of Little Rock. Winthrop acquired a herd of purebred Santa Gertrudis cattle from Robert Kleberg's King Ranch, and the cattle were the start of Winrock Farm, which is now a 34,000-acre enterprise with holdings in Arkansas and Oklahoma. He paid $31,500 for his first Santa Gertrudis bull.

Winthrop had long been a director of the National Urban League, a group designed to promote racial integration, but in the autumn of 1957, when Orval E. Faubus refused to desegregate Little Rock public schools and Dwight Eisenhower sent troops to Arkansas, Winthrop had very little to say. What he did have to say did not much help the cause of blacks. He told the *Washington Post* (October 6, 1957) that he feared business had been scared away, and he confided to the *New York Times* (September 12, 1958) that he was disappointed that Arkansas had never applied the separate-but-equal mandate.

Winthrop was defeated by Orval Faubus in the gubernatorial race in Arkansas in 1964, but in 1966 he became governor by defeating "Justice Jim" Johnson, a racist hard-liner who refused even to shake hands with black people during the campaign. Winthrop was reelected in 1968, and although he promised he would not run for more than two terms, he entered the lists again in 1970, this time meeting defeat at the hands of a reform candidate.

Winthrop first won election in 1966 by pledging prison reform. The prisons in Arkansas were the most inhuman in the country. Torture (including running electric charges through the testicles of inmates), extortion, and murder were commonplace. Winthrop said he would change all this, but things had not much changed on June 2, 1967, when Oregon Circuit Judge Lyle Wolff made an unprecedented decision: He refused to turn over four Arkansas escapees because he did not believe "the courts of Oregon should encourage Arkansas by aiding and abetting her in the management of her institutes of terror, horror, and despicable evil. No court in an asylum state has a right to ignore practices involving substantial and systematic deprivation of constitutional rights."

Judge Wolff also said that "undisputed evidence establishes that Arkansas conducts at her two penal institutions, Cummins and Tucker, a system of barbarity, cruelty, torture, bestiality, corruption, terror and animal viciousness that reeks of Dachau and Auschwitz."

Winthrop hired penologist Tom Murton to straighten matters out. Unfortunately, Murton took the governor at his word and instituted genuine reforms, reforms that injured feelings of a number of Arkansans. For example, he eliminated much of the graft that had poured money into the pockets of local entrepreneurs, and into the coffers of the state. He canceled a contract between the state of Arkansas and the Atkins Pickle Company which called for convict labor to raise a cucumber crop. He eliminated the torture and beating of convicts, which many Arkansans were for, and the segregation, which most Arkansans were for. Worst of all, he dug up the bodies of three murdered convicts and stated publicly that he would dig up others to expose past barbarities. Prison reform was fine, Winthrop thought, but he didn't need any scandals that might embarrass prominent citizens, so Tom Murton was fired. And with his dismissal, conditions in the Arkansas prisons went right back to where they had been.

Tom Murton estimated that there could have been as many as two hundred murdered inmates buried in prison fields. Toward the end of his dramatic book, *Accomplices to the Crime*, Murton makes a serious charge: "To have knowledge that a murder has been committed and not report it to the proper authorities for prosecution, subjects the individual to criminal sanctions, in Arkansas and most other states. By failing to press for the truth, for the prosecution of those who brutalized and murdered, the board of corrections and the governor of Arkansas in effect become co-conspirators and, as such, accessories after-the-fact to the crime of murder."

In 1964 Winthrop backed Barry Goldwater for president. He came out in opposition to the Federal Civil Rights Bills of 1964, 1965, and 1966. He opposes federal guidelines for school integration and in his campaigns has avoided the racial issue.

Winthrop's drinking occasionally leads to humorous situations. Speaking before the Arkansas legislature in behalf of a mixed-drink bill, Winthrop demonstrated that he genuinely believed in what he was saying. "The legislators," wrote the *Pine Bluff Commercial*, "were paying little attention to his message. They were snickering over what they assumed to be the governor's inebriation."

Rockefeller publicists claim that Winthrop has given away eight million dollars since moving to Arkansas. Perhaps. But Winthrop is probably a billionaire, and eight million dollars represents less than two months' *interest*, even at the most conservative rate of return, on a billion.

After the unhappy liaison with Bobo, Winthrop chose more carefully the second time around. He married Jeanette Edris, a hotel and theater heiress who was a divorcee with two children, and the marriage has produced three more children. Unfortunately, that union too seemed headed for divorce in 1971, when the couple announced they had separated.

Winthrop is, or has been, chairman of IBEC Housing Corporation; chairman of Winrock Enterprises, Inc.; chairman of Colonial Williamsburg, Inc.; chairman of Williamsburg Restoration, Inc.; chairman of the Arkansas Industrial Development

Commission; a director of the Union National Bank of Little Rock; a director of Rockefeller Brothers, Inc.; a director of Rockefeller Center, Inc.; and a trustee of the Rockefeller Brothers Fund and the National Fund for Medical Education.

Winthrop owns four planes, employs five pilots, has a private airfield on his ranch, and, according to *Newsweek*, has flown more than three million miles, which adds up to the equivalent of one hundred and twenty trips around the world.

Winthrop is an art collector. He has works by Henri Matisse and Maurice Utrillo. He also belongs to the finest clubs, including the Yale, Links, and Union in New York, and the Little Rock Country in Arkansas.

Which leaves David, Junior's youngest. Little has been written about his public or private life. He stays in the background, avoids publicity, is discreet, soft-spoken, self-assured. No hint of scandal touches his life. He seldom makes public pronouncements. He never seems to flex his muscles. Yet flex them he does, with shattering effect, for he is the most powerful money-man in the world.

June, 1970. I was on the phone with David's publicity man, and he sounded congenial.

"How's the book coming?" he asked.

"I haven't really written much about David yet. Mostly I've been doing family background. It's quite fascinating."

"Sure is. I've always thought of the Rockefellers as *the* American success story. You know, rags to riches, with a touch of Robin Hood at the end."

"What about David? Is he going to see me?"

"It was tricky, but I managed to fit you in. How about lunch a week from Wednesday? And you won't have to buy."

"Hey, that's great."

"Stop by my office at noon. I'll take you upstairs and introduce you."

Chapter V

→→→×←←←

"*B*EING a Rockefeller has its drawbacks," said the former Peggy McGrath, David's wife, "but I've never known David to be fussed by it. In fact, I think that he rather enjoys it."

At least as a child, David should have enjoyed it. He was born on June 12, 1915, and alternated living at four residences: a brownstone on West 54th Street; a summer home in Seal Harbor, Maine; a ranch in the Grand Teton Mountains of Wyoming; and the family estate in Pocantico Hills.

Early David realized that he was not a run-of-the-mill human. There were servants to cater to his every need, expensive games and toys and recreational facilities to keep him occupied, long talks with his father and grandfather about the responsibilities and privileges of a Rockefeller. Especially Junior, who had firsthand experience as an inheritor, lectured all his children on what they could expect from life. Although the boys were told they would not have to work to maintain themselves, they were urged from a very early day to become involved in one or another of the family enterprises.

"Appropriate" was the word most often given to Junior's children. "You must never do anything that isn't appropriate," was the lesson the young Rockefellers were most often taught.

The most "inappropriate" thing a Rockefeller could do was flaunt his wealth. To this day the Rockefellers try to handle their affairs discreetly, "appropriately," but it is almost impossible given their enormous wealth.

As a youngster, David's special value was everywhere for

him to witness. Particularly at the main mansion on the 3,500-acre estate at Pocantico Hills, which was one of John D. Rockefeller's homes until he died (then Junior moved in), and which David often visited. The main mansion was called *Kykuit*, a Dutch word meaning "lookout," and it was aptly named since it was perched on a high hill and on a clear day David could see thirty miles, past Harlem and straight to mid-Manhattan. Pocantico Hills is just east of Tarrytown in the storybook Sleepy Hollow country, a Garden of Eden sort of place where dreams became reality.

"I was fortunate to have had such a place to go to," David confided. "It was almost too beautiful, but as a boy I was never bored."

Despite long talks with John, Sr., and Junior about being appropriate and discreet, David was really the only one who practiced what he was taught. From an early age he was known as "the serious one, the scholarly one." He would retain that reputation to this day.

"Money is what the Rockefellers are all about," said a close friend of the family. "It's interesting to note that David alone became totally absorbed with the handling of money."

The other brothers would amuse themselves with politics, or "venture capitalism," or lounging around the Bahamas—pursuits that might be expected of the very rich—but David would not. Money is indeed what the Rockefellers are all about, and the fact that David is the "steward" of the family's finances, that he is *allowed* to be the steward, indicates that he is the most important of the highly important Rockefellers.

Besides the main mansion, *Kykuit*, the estate at Pocantico Hills had many other mansions and scores of buildings for maintenance and staff, plus a "playhouse" that cost one million dollars and that had bowling alleys, tennis court, squash court, swimming pool, soda fountain, card room, billiard room, and a fully equipped gymnasium. When David wasn't bowling or playing squash, he could gaze at a statue of Aphrodite, believed to be an original Praxiteles.

Merrill Folsom, author of *Great American Mansions and*

Their Stories, described the Rockefeller estate "as remote from the outside world as a fortified principality. High stone walls, massive iron gates, alert guards, police dogs and miles of barbed-wire fence make the home a sanctuary."

Actually, the barbed wire was electrified and the estate employed some thirty armed guards to keep watch at the fences in case an intruder appeared. In addition, other private police cruised the estate in radio cars, and atop *Kykuit* each night were two more armed guards manning floodlights that could illuminate the countryside for miles.

Junior had a profound fear of kidnapers, or those who nursed grudges, real or imagined, against the family. It was this fear that prompted him and his father to provide an umbrella of protection for themselves and their family that was greater than the president of the United States was receiving at the time.

"Father wouldn't even permit us to have our pictures taken," David recalled. "He thought it would be an invitation to criminals."

When David was growing up, the Pocantico Hills estate already had more than fifty miles of roads, thirty-five blooded cattle, twenty-two blooded horses, and a huge herd of sheep, which John, Sr., thought lent a pastoral setting to the place. However, the sheep unfortunately grazed on the old man's nine-hole golf course, and his drives were often stopped short by their deposits, thus making subsequent approach shots exceedingly untidy. But John, Sr., was an avid golfer and, as he proved as a businessman, hard to stop. Many times in the dead of winter he had his servants clear snow from the fairways so he could play.

Kykuit is built of granite, is four stories high, and contains fifty huge rooms. It is an Alice in Wonderland creation on an estate that requires five hundred full-time employees just to keep going. Ferdinand Lundberg wrote about *Kykuit* that "the domicile of no potentate is any better equipped."

The truth is that there is probably no domicile anywhere that is as well equipped. *Kykuit* even contains a well-stocked hospital, installed originally to keep John, Sr., alive but available to all the family members. There was also a huge pipe organ which was used to belt out religious tunes, and a complicated sound system carried the music to each of *Kykuit*'s fifty rooms.

Junior and his father made a show of religion. Both taught Sunday School, both were auspicious givers to religious causes. Theirs was the Protestant Ethic, with all it implies. They tried to instill religion in Junior's offspring, but the changing times doomed the effort to failure. Nonetheless, each Sunday Junior and his wife dressed their sons in suit and tie and starched shirt to attend services. Morning and evening prayers were required each day, and grace was regularly said at meals.

David spent a lot of time wearing a suit while he was a youngster. It was appropriate for a young Rockefeller, especially when he was taken to *Kykuit* to visit his grandfather, from whom many blessings flowed. David enjoyed *Kykuit*. It was, of course, totally air conditioned, and it was great fun to ride the elevators which whisked family members and guests to upper floors.

Even when David wanted to take a shower, he could do so in style. A family friend described the oversized marble bath, built around 1911, of *Kykuit*: "It is a truly splendid place with large brass and silver wheels which you turn to bring on and turn off various sprays, to control the force of water and of course the temperature of it. It is secure and solid and feels rather like one of those well-appointed movie submarines of pre-World War II days that had somehow got stood on end. There was one large wheel, about midsection, that I particularly liked to turn on, because I had never seen its function duplicated anywhere else. It gives you a strong, almost unbearable jet where you might expect, and the disc that fills the center of the silver wheel is marked, 'Kidney Spray.'"

The grounds around *Kykuit* were even more impressive than the inside furnishings. There were a Japanese temple and a Japanese garden, and in the garden was statuary by world-renowned George Gray Barnard. There were many other gardens—rose gardens, tulip gardens, hyacinth gardens, violet gardens, lilac gardens, hawthorn gardens—and the estate was graced with terraces, trails, portals, ponds, streams, fountains, waterfalls, bulwarks, and balustrades. Ducks and geese and other wildlife were everywhere, and there were hidden nooks and leafy bowers which provided serene settings from which to look out upon the magnificent Hudson.

Anything that offended the eyes of the Rockefellers was removed. The family took umbrage at a railroad track which paralleled the golf course and had it relocated at a cost of $700,000. Junior wanted the land St. Joe's Normal College was on, so he gave the school enough money to build a new institution. A subbasement was constructed so that garbage trucks could enter a tunnel to pick up refuse without being seen.

Just to maintain *Kykuit* cost $50,000 a year. To maintain the entire estate, which during David's growing-up years was ten times the size of Monaco and five times larger than Central Park, cost more than $500,000 and required a staff of five hundred. But Junior and his father were masters at understating their property's value and, along with temperance lectures (which David evidently did not listen to, since he is a heavy drinker), they were chiefly responsible for teaching the chairman of the board of Chase Manhattan Bank how to avoid taxes.

In 1928, when David was thirteen, the 3,500-acre estate in Pocantico Hills was valued for tax purposes at $5,588,050, a valuation that called for a total tax of $137,000. However, in 1928 the true value of the Rockefeller estate was *at least* $5,000 an acre, meaning the property had a minimum worth of $17,500,000, not including the mansions, buildings, and improvements. The May 24, 1937, issue of the *New York Times* said *Kykuit* alone had cost two million dollars to build. Nonetheless, Junior and John, Sr., were upset by the "high" valuation, and several years later had it reduced to $3,000,000.

David learned his lesson well. In 1965 the estate was valued for tax purposes at $5,115,795, less than what it was supposed to be worth in 1928, and this despite the fact that biographer

William Rodgers and others have accurately dubbed it "the most valuable residential property on earth."

In any case, in 1965 the Rockefeller land in Pocantico Hills, where all the brothers except Winthrop maintain a home, was worth a minimum of $10,000 an acre. This means the value of the estate was at least $35,000,000, not $5,115,795, and again the higher valuation doesn't include mansions, buildings, and improvements.

Trees, shrubs, and plants were brought from all over the world to the estate at Pocantico Hills. There were orange trees from the estate of Marquis d'Aux at Le Mans, France; ancient boxwoods from the Netherlands; larch from Scotland; yew from England. There were also jasmine, bay, quinces, and gingkos.

One groundsman commented that the estate "showed people what God could have done if he'd had the money."

David's boyhood years were not confined solely to Pocantico Hills. The huge residence at West 54th Street, where David stayed while he attended the Lincoln School, more resembled an art gallery than a home. It contained paintings by Picasso, Degas, Gauguin, Goya, Duccio, Botticelli, Piero della Francesca, Paolo Uccello, Fragonard, Nattier, and Chardin. In addition, there were sculptures by Laurana and Verrochio.

The home on West 54th Street, which was nine stories high, housed a huge collection of folk art, including oils, watercolors, and pastels, plus needlework, paintings on velvet and glass, and sculptures in wood and metal. If David wanted, he could study his father's collection of sixteen hundred etchings, lithographs, and woodcuts. David could also admire Junior's collection of Chinese porcelains, the finest such collection in the world and one that took an estimated $10,000,000 to accumulate.

David walked on Persian rugs, purchased from European royal families and woven of gold and silver thread, and on Persian silk rugs. If he chose to take the time, he could examine the world's finest tapestry collection, which included the famous Months of Lucas and the Hunt of the Unicorn.

Like the estate in Pocantico Hills, the home on West 54th Street had a well-equipped gymnasium. There was also an open-air roof playground, plus an ice-skating rink and an infirmary. For less vigorous pursuits David could go to the home's enormous record library or book library.

"Father wanted us to grow up in a cultured atmosphere," David said, but that was hardly Junior's reason (at least where paintings were concerned) for overflowing the West 54th Street home with art treasures.

Junior was no art connoisseur. He relied almost exclusively on the advice of experts. Nevertheless, he had learned early what the *Wall Street Journal* got around to revealing on January 3, 1967: "Art is a growth stock, a whopping tax deduction.

"The rise in prices," the *Journal* continued, "has led many purchasers to view art as an instrument whose growth potential puts many a high-flying stock to shame. According to dealers and others in the art world, some 'collectors' who not long ago thought Modigliani was some kind of Italian dish, now move in and out of the art market like so many Wall Street speculators, hunting bargains, and then trying to resell them at a fancy price."

Even more common, however, is the use of paintings as a tax deduction, a trick Junior learned early and one that David has been copying. Here's the way it works: A man buys a painting for $10,000, holds it awhile, then gives it to a museum stating that its value is now $50,000. Thus he has earned a $40,000 deduction from taxable income, along with earning the gratitude of an uninformed public who feel the "giver" has donated a valuable work of art to mankind. The museum, of course, grateful for the painting, is not going to question its value, nor is anyone else, since value where paintings are concerned is pretty much a subjective matter. This was a stunt Junior used often, helping relieve what he considered an unfair tax burden.

The *Wall Street Journal* reported that IRS, after studying a number of such donations, "found that the art objects had cost the donors a total of $1,471,502—but that their declared 'fair market value' had climbed to $5,811,908."

In 1959 David helped authorize Chase Manhattan Bank's "art program." Since then more than fifteen hundred paintings have been purchased, at prices ranging between $100 and $10,000, and the paintings are scattered throughout dozens of locations in New York City and in some twenty branch banks overseas. The paintings represent the works of artists from forty different countries and date from pre-Columbian times to the present. David said that the reason for buying the paintings was "to give maximum enrichment and decoration to the whole series of environments in which we and our customers do business."

That's not the whole story. At a 1970 stockholders' meeting, when it was suggested that David was throwing away money that could be used to pay dividends, he hastily answered that the Chase's investment in paintings had appreciated considerably. He didn't add that a number of them had already found their way into museums.

David has also acquired an art collection of his own. Part of it he received after his aunt, Lucy Aldrich, died in 1956. The family sat around drawing lots for Aunt Lucy's many treasures, and David won a number of her Asian objets d'art and half of her library. Of course, David himself is a major "giver" to museums.

Incidentally, Lucy Aldrich shared Junior's views on taxation. In a letter to David's mother, she wrote, "I have had the most wonderful time with your children, your most valuable possessions. One thing that Roosevelt can't do is put a tax on them."

One of the more exciting events of David's childhood occurred when he was eight. Aunt Lucy was kidnaped while visiting China and held for a weekend by bandits. The family was afraid they would have to pay ransom, but she was rescued.

David's third boyhood home, usually occupied only in the

summer, was at Seal Harbor, on Mount Desert Island in Maine. The family called the place a "cottage," but it had ninety rooms. There the Rockefeller family maintained a flotilla of seagoing vessels, including half a dozen yachts.

As an adult David has accumulated his own fleet of power and sailing ships, some of which, in his spare moments, he has navigated as far away as St. Bart's in the French West Indies and St. Croix in the Virgin Islands. One supership of David's, which he co-owned with brothers Nelson and Laurance, required a full-time staff of a captain and five crewmen. David's son, David, Jr., has also become an avid seaman. He has participated in America's Cup competition as a crewman.

In some ways David was much like any other little boy. At age three, after spotting a dead whale on the beach at Seal Harbor, he asked Junior if he could venture closer to get a better look. Junior said no, and David began to cry. "All my life," he said, stomping his feet, "I've never seen a whale."

David's fourth boyhood home, the ranch in the Grand Teton Mountains, was located on 30,000 acres of land that Junior owned. The ranch was situated in an area so beautiful that it was later made part of the magnificent Grand Teton National Park.

As a boy David was average in height but quite obese. At age five, when he wanted to roller skate from the 54th Street home to the Lincoln School, Junior had him trailed by a nurse on foot, in case he got winded, and by an armed guard in a limousine, lest he be kidnaped. Most of the time, however, David pulled up to the doors of the school in the limousine.

Even at age five David had been taught not to flaunt the family's wealth. Especially at the Lincoln School, which a number of children from low-income families attended. "Is it true," David was asked by a classmate, "that your grandfather is the richest man in the world?"

"Certainly not," replied the five-year-old. "Henry Ford is much richer."

At age thirteen David still had a weight problem. Trying to

ascend a pyramid on a visit to Egypt, he needed the help of two guides, one pushing and the other pulling, to get to the top.

David's average during twelve years at the Lincoln School was only B-minus, but he was getting an outside education that few children in the world enjoy. All around him were priceless art treasures, and the people who visited his father, and chatted with him, were almost inevitably brilliant and successful. David's environment was patrician and cultured; he was never allowed to forget that he was being groomed to lead, that it was his birthright to lead. Like a descendant of royalty, David never questioned his birthright.

Another part of David's education was the travel. On the trip to Egypt he also visited Palestine, Syria, and Lebanon, cruising up the Nile in a chartered boat. David was accompanied on the trip by a private tutor, and also along were a doctor, secretary, maid, and valet. The tour's personal guide was Dr. James H. Breasted, the University of Chicago scholar who was the first full-fledged American professor of Egyptology.

David visited France when he was eleven years old, making up for a trip he had missed when he was seven. On the earlier jaunt his mother had taken her daughter Abby and her son Winthrop, while the three older boys had cavorted with Junior in Montana. David, having been judged too young, was left in New York with a tutor.

David also traveled extensively in the United States. At age seven he made his first of many tours of the country, in a private railroad car the family owned. The car cost $125,000, and required an additional $50,000 a year to maintain. At age eleven David was with his father on Junior's first visit to Williamsburg, Virginia. He was a serious youngster, took an interest in what Junior was planning in Williamsburg, made such an impression on some of the local residents that when they wrote to Junior they addressed their correspondence to "David's Father."

Junior was constantly throwing parties (a habit David has copied), and a letter from his wife to one of her sons described the hectic pace the Rockefeller family maintained: "I am going to Philadelphia tomorrow to see the Persian exhibit, and Commander Byrd is coming to tea so I must be back at five o'clock. Tuesday the Batchelders are coming to visit us for three days, and Tuesday evening Dr. Breasted is giving a lecture here to about a hundred people. He will stay here, too. Wednesday we are all dining out, and on Thursday we are giving a big party. On Friday you come—how glad we shall be to see you and that day is yours!—but on Saturday evening we must again have dinner away from home."

Notwithstanding the furious social pace his parents maintained, David's childhood could best be called protected. David's friends were mostly well-bred sons of the upper class. He did not roughhouse in sandlots or go to neighborhood movies on Saturday afternoons. In fact, a good deal of his time was spent attending Bible classes. He also remembers sitting on his grandfather's knee and reciting a poem:

> *Five cents a glass, does anyone think*
> *That that is really the price of a drink?*
> *The price of a drink, let him decide*
> *Who has lost his courage and his pride,*
> *And who lies a grovelling heap of clay*
> *Not far removed from a beast today.*

Just as Junior had been raised in a hothouse atmosphere, so too was David. Junior, and especially John, Sr., wanted it that way. They wanted to raise a businessman, a leader, a tiger in the mold of the grandfather, to take over the handling of the family fortune. They also wanted David to be suave, cool, sophisticated. The days of the robber barons were past. A new sort of corporate titan was needed.

It is true that David's brothers were groomed the same way he was, but it turned out that they didn't (with the possible exception of Laurance) make it in the rough and tumble of high finance. Only David, the youngest, would prove worthy to travel in the wake of his grandfather.

Rockefeller business associates treated young David with the sort of reverence generally reserved for royalty. Servants were always on hand to do his bidding, to make sure that his needs were quickly satisfied. Giving orders, in the form of polite requests, was second nature for David before he even entered school. The granting of requests, unless specifically forbidden by Junior, was always carried out with a minimum of fuss, with amazing dispatch.

David was a genial youngster, open and friendly, and he addressed his parents as "Father" and "Mother." Courtesy to one's parents was mandatory in the Rockefeller home. The fact that the world was one's oyster was taken for granted. David was a nice young man who was aware that some day, if not immediately, he could have anything he wanted.

But David would prove different from his brothers. Friends say that it was because he was the youngest and still under Junior's roof when his brothers were gone away, and that Junior, realizing that he had gone wrong somewhere, spent additional time drilling David in the behavior expected of the genteel, yet powerful, rich.

Nelson, Laurance, and Winthrop broke loose as soon as they left their father's home. All were interested in drinking, in the pleasure of women, in fun-type living. John III, although of a different bent, was certainly not the business/aristocrat Junior had hoped for.

Whatever else David became, he became a hard and conscientious worker. "He has a compulsion to be overcommitted," said his wife Peggy. "I would question his judgment about how much he takes on. I, being lazy, enjoy things like slopping around in boats. But he enjoys being busy every single minute. Everybody else around him gets tired, but he doesn't."

What makes David run so hard?

"I think," said Peggy, "he wants to prove to himself and to the world that a Rockefeller doesn't have to be a spoiled s.o.b."

As a youngster David's weight discouraged participation in

many boyhood activities. His chief hobby, begun when he was a fifth grader at the Lincoln School, was collecting beetles, and the hobby has remained his avocation to the present day.

David spent two youthful summers in Maine hobnobbing with Henry Ford II, chasing beetles, and, according to a family historian, "studying nature." Today David has more than 40,000 beetle specimens, which he keeps in an air-conditioned basement room at his home in Pocantico Hills. Bank presidents and presidents of countries send him specimens in a variety of containers.

"The rule," said one of his secretaries, Edna Bruderle, "is to cut the string and stand back."

Wherever David goes, he carries several glass bottles with stoppers and a supply of cotton and formaldehyde. The collection has grown so large, and he has become so busy, that he employs a two-day-a-week beetle curator to keep his collection in order.

Beetles are a passion with David. He has been known to leave important receptions unexpectedly to hunt them down. "He has me so indoctrinated," said his son David, Jr., who collects bottle caps, "that I sometimes dream about them."

One guest was having cocktails at David's Pocantico Hills mansion when a black bug settled on his host's forehead. David let the bug sit there for awhile, then picked it off and made an examination. "Member of the *Scolytidae* family," he observed, before letting the creature loose.

As a youngster, David abandoned his beetle collection for two summers to study the color perceptivity of bees at the Museum of Natural History for the Study of Insects, but beetles were his true love and he returned to them. Today two beetles, the *Acmaeodera rockefelleri* and the *Cicendela rockefelleri* are named after him.

David had plenty of ways to keep himself amused as a youngster, but he did not have a lot of cash to throw around. Junior thought he should learn the value of money early. David's allowance in his first years of grade school was 25 cents a week, and he had to spend eight hours raking leaves to get that. He could earn extra money pulling weeds, one cent for each weed pulled. However, David was required to keep track of every expenditure he made, jotting down the amounts and reasons for each one in a notebook which Junior checked faithfully each week. David was forced to pay a fine whenever a mistake was discovered.

"Father taught us that excess (!) of any kind was intolerable for a Rockefeller," David said. "His strict rule was that we should save ten percent of our money and give away ten percent."

As mentioned, the Rockefellers had a flotilla of expensive boats, but when David took it upon himself to order a toy sailboat on his tenth birthday, Junior deducted the $4 cost from his allowance. On another occasion, when asked by a friend why he didn't have a certain expensive item, David replied, "Who do you think we are, the Vanderbilts?"

The Lincoln School that David attended used the progressive techniques of philosopher John Dewey. "The progressive education," said David, "was an exhilarating experience. The idea was to fire our imagination, and I think it worked." David hesitated a moment, then added ruefully, "It failed to teach me to read fast or to spell correctly, and I've never been very good at either."

At least where reading is concerned, David has not found it necessary to be fast. "None of us," he said, referring to himself and his brothers, "have ever found much time to read. I guess we've just been too busy with other things."

David's early years may have influenced a statement he made in 1968 to the Federal Equal Employment Opportunity Commission: "Economic development—whether in Harlem or Haiti—is essentially a do-it-yourself proposition. True, business can and must assist in every way possible. But the basic drive and determination must come from within the Negro and Spanish American communities themselves."

So spoke David Rockefeller, the inheritor, telling blacks and Spanish-speaking Americans that success is primarily a pull-yourself-up-by-the-bootstraps enterprise.

I wore a sports shirt and unpressed pants. I had wanted to dress more formally for the occasion but my publisher, Lyle Stuart, had nixed the idea.

"You never dress up when you come to see me," Stuart had said.

"This is different," I said. "I'd better look straight."

"You're a writer, not a banker. Go as you are."

"If I go like this, he'll probably throw me out."

"After he talks with you, he may throw you out anyway. Go as you are."

So I went as I was.

Chapter VI

—»>)«<«—

"*H*E WAS a pudgy seventeen," said a friend of the family, recalling when David entered Harvard, "and every ambitious mother in Boston was pushing her daughter at him." ·

David entered Harvard in 1932, and ever since Rockefeller publicists have hailed him as a mental giant, an intellectual titan, a Mount Everest of academic achievement. Even some of his competitors agree: "We have very few real intellectuals on Wall Street," the president of a rival bank told the *New Yorker*, "but David is one of them."

David is indeed an extremely bright man (he wouldn't be handling the family's money if he wasn't), but his genius wasn't evident at Harvard, where in four undergraduate years he received only one "A," and that in an entomology course taught by William Martin Wheeler, an ant specialist.

David's interest in entomology dawned at the age of ten, he carried it into adult life, and he maintains it today. An observer might find it fascinating to speculate on the possibilities opened up by that lone undergraduate "A" at Harvard. Had a guidance counselor told David he showed a definite talent and preference for this particular biological field, the story of the powerful Chase Manhattan Bank might be somewhat different. This most educated of the Rockefellers could well have bloomed as an entomologist and made his career in the academic world, perhaps ending up as a college professor. But no such suggestion was ever seriously given to David, nor would it have been welcome at Pocantico Hills, where the hopes of the family rested so heavily on the youngest son.

David's undergraduate years at Harvard could only be termed undistinguished. His name wasn't even mentioned in the Harvard yearbooks of 1933, 1934, and 1935, although this fact alone reveals very little. Acknowledging that J. Robert Oppenheimer, the brilliant theoretical physicist, had attended Harvard, the yearbooks mentioned him only once, and then to say he had been "in college three years as an undergraduate."

David lived at Eliot House, the swankiest and most expensive residence at Harvard. Here's the way the 1936 yearbook described the place: "Rambling along the Charles, Eliot, newest and biggest of the houses, resembles an overgrown apartment house whose architect, misled by delusions of grandeur, inserted elephantine scrolls at random and topped his work with a grotesque baroque tower."

David wasn't even one of the more distinguished members of Eliot House. The 1936 Harvard yearbook, in describing Eliot, listed dozens of residents, but not Junior's youngest, which seems strange, since the presence of a Rockefeller should warrant at least a footnote. David did, however, take part in a drive to collect money for clothes for impoverished residents of Labrador. After "persistent efforts," a total of $125 was raised for the Labradorians.

David majored in history and literature and during his freshman year took part in intramural golf, soccer, and squash.

There were no blacks in David's graduating class, but there were plenty of the sons of the rich. Theodore Roosevelt III was a classmate. There was also a Pabst, a McAlpine, a Fitzgerald (Kennedy family), a Pulitzer, a Whitney, a Goodyear, and a Ballantine.

David would later become one of the most important spokesmen for the rich. He would oppose Minimum Wage legislation, less stringent bank credit policies toward lower income borrowers, the 35-hour workweek. His attitude was understandable, of course. He understood the problems of the wealthy, sympathized with them, related to them. After all, he himself was wealthy, and his entire life was spent with other people of means.

It was at a dance during his freshman year that David met his bride-to-be, Margaret "Peggy" McGrath, a student at the Chapin School. Peggy's father was a member of the prestigious law firm of Cadwalader, Wickersham & Taft, whose offices were at 14 Wall Street.

"Peggy was plenty impressed by the Rockefeller wealth," said a man who once dated her, "but you should have seen her parents. They were drooling over the prospect of their daughter marrying all that money."

David and Peggy McGrath saw a lot of each other during David's years at Harvard. Mostly they had dancing dates, and Peggy says "he is still the dreamiest waltzer in the world."

When David graduated from Harvard in 1936 he was uncertain about what he should do for a career, so he went for advice to Junior's closest friend, Canada's late Prime Minister William Lyon MacKenzie King. (Their friendship notwithstanding, Junior and the prime minister always addressed each other as "Mr. King" and "Mr. Rockefeller.")

Prime Minister King advised David to continue his education, preferably in economic and foreign affairs. King knew about the Rockefeller family's interest in the Chase. He also knew that David intended to work for one or another of his grandfather's businesses. Banking, he told David, was the most important of all businesses.

David took King's advice and enrolled in graduate courses at Harvard, but later he had reason to question the counsel he had received. Upon King's death it was revealed that when *he* needed advice he turned to a spiritualist, who put him in touch with his dead mother via séances.

David spent a year in graduate school at Harvard, and among his classmates was economist Paul Samuelson. "Samuelson was by all odds the star of the class," said David. "He was pretty far to the left, though of course he has matured and moderated his views since then."

David liked the academic atmosphere, the pace was leisurely, scholarly, and in 1938 he decided to go to England to study at the Rockefeller-supported London School of Economics. David kept in touch with Peggy by running up astronomical phone bills, and became acquainted with John Kennedy, whose father was then ambassador to the Court of St. James. In addition, David had several dates with Joe Kennedy's daughter, Kathleen.

David received his first taste of banking while in London. His uncle, Winthrop Aldrich, was chairman of the board of the Chase Bank, and David spent several hours each week in its London branch.

David stayed only one year in England. Then he returned to the States and enrolled at the Rockefeller-founded University of Chicago where, in the summer of 1940, he was awarded his doctorate in economics. He received the degree *in absentia*, since he had come home to New York in the spring of that year.

Since he was a Rockefeller, any story about David was news, and when he didn't have fifteen cents to pay for the use of a University of Chicago tennis court in 1939, the item was printed in newspapers across the country.

David's graduation with a doctorate in economics culminated eight years of higher education. He was indeed "the serious one," the one who could be counted on to oversee the family's farflung empire.

David's doctoral thesis, *Unused Resources and Economic Waste*, was a 229-page defense of the status quo, although one sentence in the thesis probably made his grandfather turn in his grave: "The existence of monopoly offers *prima-facie* evidence of a social evil."

The thesis was, expectedly, antiunion. It contended that "the raising of wages and the shortening of hours through wage and hour legislation had forced employers to use mechanical substitutes for manual labor and to discharge people."

The thesis also attacked the National Labor Relations Board

and high taxes against the rich, "which approach confiscation in the higher brackets."

David described Peggy's reaction to his thesis: "I began reading it to her, but she fell asleep after the third page. I guess it isn't exactly light reading."

When David returned to New York City from Chicago in the spring of 1940, he showed he was in favor of the poor by visiting the Municipal Lodging House, a home for the unemployed, at 432 East 25th Street. David's visit was accorded considerable fanfare by the New York press, who were impressed by the fact that he had ridden the subway to get to the home and that he had eaten the same six-and-a-half-cent meal of corn soup and codfish that the residents had. At the end of his visit, David begged off posing for pictures with those who lived in the shelter.

Columnist Ernest Meyer, commenting on David's visit to the Municipal Lodging House, wrote that "one hopes that on the basis of having eaten codfish with lodgers in a free flophouse, Mr. Rockefeller will not feel qualified to write a long and scholarly dissertation on what it means and how it feels to be poor."

To David's credit, no such dissertation was written.

The day of the visit to the Municipal Lodging House was a busy one for David. That evening he and Peggy entered a polka contest at Junior's Rainbow Room in Manhattan and danced off with first prize.

David married Peggy McGrath on September 7, 1940, and the event was one of the big social occasions of the year, a must for the yachting and polo set (in 1970 there were thirty-six Rockefellers in the New York Social Register alone).

The wedding took place at historic Saint Matthews Protestant Episcopal Church, built in 1803 by John Jay, first chief justice of the United States Supreme Court; and some two hundred and fifty people crowded into the tiny chapel. Things were so cramped that there wasn't room for the bridal party to line up in back before going down the aisle.

The color scheme used for the wedding was white and yellow, and Peggy was bedecked with pearls and a large brooch of diamonds and platinum. She wore a square-necked ivory satin princess gown and carried a bouquet of lilies-of-the-valley and orchids.

John III was David's best man, and Nelson, Laurance, and Winthrop were ushers. Although only two hundred and fifty had been able to squeeze into the small church, nearly a thousand guests attended the lavish reception at The Narrows, the Mount Kisco home of Peggy's parents, Mr. and Mrs. Francis Sims McGrath.

Peggy McGrath Rockefeller, at the time of her marriage, was slim, dark-haired, clear-eyed, a very pretty post-debutante. Today she is interested in music and gardening, and she has financed this country's most comprehensive study of wild flowers. Four volumes, costing thirty dollars each, have already been published, and four more are planned.

Peggy Rockefeller is a Society Wife, and not the kind who dominates the pages of *Town and Country*, or pops up in *Vogue* with the dismal regularity of the café society set. Rather she has tended to her gentlewoman's interests behind the trimmed, high hedges of her husband's estates. She is not photographed debarking from planes, or dodging out of restaurants.

"Quite frankly," says a family observer, "Peggy is a snob. She knows how important her husband is, and that makes her feel important. At least David makes an effort to show that he's just common folk. Peggy doesn't bother to try."

Peggy Rockefeller has a sharp tongue and dislikes a number of people, Jacqueline Onassis in particular, whom she attacks with the bone-grazing deftness of a piranha.

She can be cruel to those who do not meet her standards of what is beautiful or appropriate. "That woman!" she was heard to exclaim about an elderly neighbor. "Where does she get those ideas about gardening? She must be part gypsy!"

Peggy's distaste for cameras and publicity, coupled with her low-key private life, has spared her the ordeal of being recognized on the streets of New York during her occasional forays into the city. Her name, however, is another matter, as she found out the day she wandered into Alexander's, a medium-priced department store, and decided to charge something she liked.

"My God," whispered the flabbergasted clerk as she read the famous name. "Are you *the* Rockefeller?"

Peggy didn't bat an eye. "Whom, may I ask, do you consider to be *the* Rockefeller?"

Peggy has tried her hand at music publishing, but she had to give it up when the venture started to make money. The company she had formed was supposed to be nonprofit.

Peggy likes to chug around in her Model T Ford, to travel, to tend her greenhouse, to sail, to raise redwoods. She has given David six children—David, Jr., Abby, Neva (Mrs. Walter J. Kaiser), Margaret, Richard, and Eileen.

At least one of David's children has grown to adulthood outside the accepted Establishment mold. His daughter Abby has been active in the Women's Liberation movement, and a picture of her giving karate lessons was printed in a variety of newspapers.

After leaving the University of Chicago, David had gone to work as a secretary for Mayor Fiorello LaGuardia and, when his honeymoon ended, he returned to that post. David served on LaGuardia's staff without pay, and his main contribution to the city's welfare was the sale of $6,000 worth of rental space at LaGuardia Field to five New York City firms. On another occasion, when the mayor wanted to invite a couple dozen Latin Americans to study for a year at New York colleges, David persuaded a number of corporations to contribute a thousand dollars apiece for that purpose. There were few major companies that would refuse to open their doors to someone named Rockefeller.

"City Hall, Rockefeller speaking," was the way David answered the phone, until LaGuardia told him to cut it out.

After receiving his doctorate, David was 90 percent sure that he would join the Chase bank. But in keeping with a family custom that is still honored, he decided first to put in some time in public service. Many of the Rockefellers, before and since, have done precisely this, working with VISTA or the Peace Corps, before going on to high-paying positions in the family's businesses. Some of the Rockefellers have been genuinely motivated. Others saw it as a method to project a favorable image.

David's first son, David, Jr., was born on July 24, 1941, in the Harkness Pavilion of the Columbia-Presbyterian Medical Center.

David resigned his job with LaGuardia on September 30, 1941, to become assistant regional director of the United States Office of Defense, Health and Welfare Services, where he was under the supervision of Anna Rosenberg.

David enlisted in the Army in May, 1942, and took basic training at Governors Island. His original plan was to serve as an enlisted man, but a taste of barracks life and the smell of a GI who tended the colonel's horses—"I couldn't breathe," said David—convinced him that Officer Candidate School was the place to be. David could speak French (he also speaks Spanish and German), and in 1943 he was sent to Algiers as an intelligence officer.

David's position in the U.S. Army was probably unique. His duties in Algeria consisted almost solely of keeping in touch with representatives of the French Free Government so he could learn what the Nazis had done with various Rockefeller family properties, especially art treasures the Germans had stolen. Eighteen months later, after Paris was liberated, the then Captain Rockefeller was assigned to the U.S. Embassy in France, again as an intelligence officer.

"All David did in Paris," remarked an officer who served with him, "was chase around the countryside tracking down family belongings. We liked to kid him, saying that he was on the first jeep into Paris after the Nazis were out."

Actually, the only action David saw in France was at the Officers' Club, where he was either being flattered by sycophants or derided by those unimpressed by his name.

Generals were the ones who most fawned over Junior's youngest. They were constantly buying him drinks, inviting him to dinner, treating him as though he were Commander-in-Chief.

David knew how to deal with the generals. Their sort had always been around the mansion in Pocantico Hills and the home on West 54th Street. David considered himself their superior, as indeed did they.

David's critics were something else. Except for a few speeches he had given to Depression-ridden Chicago while he had been a student there, he had not been exposed to outright hostility, and he was not sure how to react when faced with it. Some of David's fellow officers resented the special treatment he received, the relatively soft job he had. A few of the more bitter intimated that his family was profiting from the war. Nevertheless, it is to David's credit that some of the officers who rode him most relentlessly became his friends, and are now high-paid employees of the Chase Manhattan Bank.

French leaders regarded David as an "ambassador without portfolio," but that didn't endear him to the French people. "The average citizen," said Dick Dana, now one of David's top aides, "was anti-American and anti-Rockefeller."

David's favorite hangout in Paris was the Officers' Club, where he developed a reputation for hearty drinking. If anything, he drinks more today. He says the enormous burdens of the bank, with its farflung investments, make him tense, that alcohol relaxes him.

Today David has an elaborate collection of wines, which he keeps in a cellar that has a bank-vault door and its own temperature-control system. The wine cellar adjoins the beetle room at his Pocantico Hills home.

"He's a little stronger in Burgundies than I am, I guess," said William A. M. Burden, a descendant of the Vanderbilts, "but I'm probably a little stronger in Bordeaux."

In a 1970 appearance on the David Frost Show, when asked what people give the man who has everything, David replied that his best friends send him wine. He is also a shareholder in La Societé Viticole du Chateau Lascombes, a Bordeaux vineyard.

While attached to the U.S. Embassy in Paris, David developed an appreciation for French cuisine, and today there is little that can keep him from enjoying a good meal when he's in France. In 1958, during the height of the Algerian crisis, with Paris rife with rumors of paratroops dropping from the skies, David passed lines of armed soldiers and gendarmes in riot garb to reach the Grand Vefour, one of his favorite restaurants. Many of David's associates were too frightened to eat, but he attacked his meal with the gusto of a starving man.

David is conscientious about his weight problem, so to accommodate his drinking he eats only one large meal a day. Breakfast, usually eaten at home, consists of orange juice, cereal, and coffee; lunch, taken at the bank's executive dining room where menus list the calorie value of each item, often means a lamb chop, salad, and fruit; dinner, again usually at home and always preceded by a number of martinis, might feature a slice of prime beef or a fine steak. During dinner there is always a large selection of wines from which to choose. David is so fond of wine, in fact, that he made plans for a wine museum in San Francisco.

After V-J Day, while David was still in Paris, Uncle Winthrop, Chase's chairman, arrived in France and asked his nephew if he was ready to join the bank. David said he was.

David was released from the Army in December, 1945, and although his combat experience was nil he was awarded the Legion of Merit, the Commendation Ribbon, and the French Legion of Honor.

In April, 1946, David went to work for the Chase, starting, as Junior proudly noted, "on the bottom."

"Here I am," I told the p.r. man. He sat in the same spiffy office and sported the same bow tie. I sensed that he was less than happy to see me.

"Mr. Hoffman. I've been trying to reach you. Evidently your telephone is unlisted."

"I don't have a telephone."

"Oh."

"What's the problem? I hope David hasn't canceled out."

"It was on my recommendation. And I think you know why."

I thought I did. But I didn't say anything.

"Frankly," Bow Tie continued, "we don't think this book is going to be in Mr. Rockefeller's best interests."

"I don't see how you can say that until you've seen it."

"What you wrote about John MacArthur wasn't pleasant. *The Stockholder,* wasn't that the name of the book?"

It was. And I had the feeling that I'd better think of something—fast—or I wasn't going to see David at all.

Chapter VII

꠸꠸꠸

*I*N *1961* Bernard Newman, a New York County Republican leader, said that David would be an excellent candidate for mayor because he was "a self-made man." Few self-made men have reaped the honors Junior's youngest has.

David is, or has been, chairman of the Chase Manhattan Bank; chairman of the Chase International Investment Corporation; chairman of Morningside Heights, Inc.; chairman of the Rockefeller Brothers Fund; chairman of the Museum of Modern Art; chairman of Rockefeller University; chairman of the International Executive Service Corps; vice chairman of the business and finance committee of the Mayor's Advisory Committee in New York City; president of the Sealantic Fund; president of the Board of Overseers of Harvard; vice president and director of the Council on Foreign Relations; a director of B. F. Goodrich Company; a director of International Basic Economy Corporation; a director of Punta Alegre Sugar Corporation; a director of American Overseas Finance Corporation; a director of the Laboratory for Electronics, Inc.; a director of the World's Fair Corporation; a trustee and chairman of the executive committee of International House; a trustee of the Carnegie Endowment for International Peace; a trustee of the University of Chicago; a trustee of the John F. Kennedy Library; a member of the Westchester County Planning Commission; a member of the United Nations Advisory Board of the Staff Pension Fund; a partner in L'Enfant Plaza, a $65,000,000 office-hotel complex in Washington, D.C.; a partner in Embarcadero Center, a $125,000,000 office-hotel complex in San Francisco; a partner in a 4,000-acre resort development in St. Croix, Virgin Islands; a partner in a cattle ranch in Argentina; and a partner in a 15,500-acre sheep ranch in Australia.

David is the recipient of an honorary LL.D. degree from Columbia University; the Award of Merit from the American Institute of Architects; the West Side Association of Commerce's City Award; the Citizens Budget Commission's medal for high civic service; the World Brotherhood Award of the Jewish Theological Seminary of America; the Medal of Honor of the St. Nicholas Society; the Scroll of Honor of the Municipal Art Society; the New York Board of Trade's Outstanding Civic Program Award; *Saturday Review's* Businessman of the Year Award (1965); the National Institute of Social Sciences Distinguished Service to Humanity Award; and the Order of the Cruz of Boyaca of Colombia.

David's rise to the top of Chase Manhattan Bank is just as stirring as the awards he has received. He started as an assistant manager in the foreign department in 1946; he was assistant cashier in 1947; second vice president, 1948; vice president, 1949; senior vice president, 1952; executive vice president, 1955; vice chairman of the board of directors, 1957; president and chairman of the executive committee, 1960; chairman of the board, 1969.

But long before David was chairman of the board he was running the show at Chase Manhattan. George Champion, who preceded him as chairman, was an able banker but a member of the old school, not fully capable of envisioning the huge profits to be realized in overseas expansion. Champion was a figurehead and he knew it. Even if his shortcomings were disregarded, the Chase was still a family bank and the Rockefellers wanted a blood relative running it. Besides, David had been raised to rule, to command, to keep the Rockefeller fortune intact and growing. George Champion was aware that he was simply someone filling in long enough so that any disgruntled stockholder crying "nepotism" could be shown that it took David twenty-three years to reach the top.

Few people were confused about who wielded the real power at the Chase. In fact, as early as 1954, the *New York Post* had gleaned the truth concerning David's future. Reporting on a speech he delivered, the *Post* said:

"There was more than just a speech involved in the talk of David Rockefeller before the oil men in Chicago.

"The talk was interesting. But more interesting is his introduction on the national scene, for he is being groomed for the presidency of the country's third biggest bank [it is now second biggest]—the Chase National.

"This youngest son of John D. Rockefeller, Jr., is now senior vice president of the Chase. He is 39. The Rockefellers are the dominant interest in the bank, and David Rockefeller's uncle, Winthrop Aldrich, who married John D. Jr.'s sister, headed the bank until his appointment as ambassador to the Court of St. James.

"When David becomes in time the top man at Chase, there will be two Rockefellers at the head of New York's two biggest banks. Stillman Rockefeller is president of the National City."

If in 1954 everyone did not recognize that David was the power at the Chase, he proved his influence a year later by persuading the directors to undertake the $125,000,000 construction of the Chase Manhattan Bank Plaza.

David was the moving force behind the Chase Manhattan Bank Plaza. Most of the directors thought it was too expensive, that it wasn't necessary, that it would be built in an area (downtown Manhattan) that other businesses were fleeing from. But David was the bank's largest stockholder and his family controlled the place, so he had the final say.

Chase Manhattan Bank Plaza is a magnificent building. It was completed in 1961, towers sixty-four stories high, has eighty-eight hundred oversized windows and five basement floors (the lowest contains the largest bank vault on earth). Outside is an oasis of green, with trees and a Japanese pool.

David has had the Chase Manhattan Bank Plaza filled with

paintings that have been selected by a committee including: Alfred H. Barr, Jr., director of collections at the Modern Museum; Robert B. Hale, of the Metropolitan Museum of Art; Perry T. Rathbone, of the Boston Museum of Fine Arts; James Joseph Sweeney, formerly of the Guggenheim Museum; and Gordon Bunshaft, an architect with Skidmore, Owings & Merrill.

Although a bank rule stipulates that, in order to preserve the building's aesthetic harmony, no employees may exhibit their own art objects or paintings, David has exempted himself from the regulation. The *New Yorker* described the office where he works:

"In his own office, on the seventeenth floor—a twenty-six-by-twenty-seven-foot chamber with a push-button-operated opaque-glass sliding door to shield him from sightseers—he has a large abstract oil by Kenzo Okada, a Wyeth, a Signac, a Cézanne watercolor, a Mark Rothko, and, perhaps his favorite, a bold Victor Vasarely. He also has some Greek vases of the fifth century B.C., a wooden Buddha, a Chinese lacquered chest, a twelfth century Mosul incense burner, some Korean acrobats carved out of wood (his mother gave them to him when he was in college, and they have been talismans ever since), a Cézanne lithograph, a glass-faced sheet of small buddhas, which were given to him by a Prince of Thailand (the Japanese royal family had presented this to the Thai royal family, and the Prince passed it along to what struck him as a prince of a comparable American tribe), and a sumgbolo—a carved wooden box from the Ivory Coast."

Outside David's office, in a glass case, are the pistols used in the Hamilton-Burr duel. Incidentally, all the works of art and artifacts in David's office are his personal possessions.

The many boards David sits on, the awards he has received, his rapid promotions at the Chase, the enormous influence he wielded, even from the first, the royal atmosphere of his office —all these things and more indicate that Junior's youngest is something more than a bank executive. Which indeed he is.

He is an American aristocrat, an upper-upper member of the upper class—according to his nephew, John IV, "probably the most powerful man in America."

David is not at all awed by his position. It was understood from the beginning that he would be a mover and shaker, and he accepts the fact as calmly as another man might acknowledge the ownership of an automobile. Nor is David shaken by the charge that he is an inheritor of tainted wealth. "He figures," said a family friend, "that the money has to be in someone's hands. Better the Rockefellers, he believes, than people who might fritter it away on foolish projects. If you question him closely, he'll always come back to the philanthropies. Then he'll ask what other family would give what his has."

David is a very serious man. He takes himself as seriously as he takes the world he lives in. He seldom jokes or makes light remarks. He speaks quietly, as one can when he knows he'll be listened to. He is cool. He is as much into foreign relations as any government and realizes that firebrand rhetoric doesn't solve ticklish problems. He also realizes that the nationalization of a Peruvian oil well, or the election of a Chilean Marxist president, or the overthrow of a neutralist Middle East chieftain, can set off a chain of results that could prove disastrous to his family's empire. So he is serious, thoughtful, careful; he can be tough when he has to be. He is involved primarily in two areas, politics and economics, with the emphasis on the former. The emphasis is not one of choice, but David is aware that under a different political system he would be just another citizen.

Just as David has proved to be a master at understating the value of the Pocantico Hills estate, so too is he adept at undervaluing the property of Chase Manhattan Bank. Chase's 1969 annual report stated that the total value of all the buildings and equipment it owns is $173,982,831.

This is a laughably low estimate. The Chase owns some of the most sophisticated computer equipment in the world. The

Chase Manhattan Bank Plaza alone is worth more than $173,982,831, not to mention Chase's many branch bank buildings throughout New York City.

An example of the power of David and the Chase Manhattan Bank, and one of the reasons Chase through its combined trust departments has the minority controlling interest in Trans World Airlines, occurred in 1960 and involved Howard Hughes.

Howard Hughes, who is called the richest man in the world but who is actually far down on the totem pole where *power* is concerned, had to have money—lots of it—to purchase the jet planes TWA needed to keep pace with its competitors. Hughes had acquired control of TWA when it was a small, struggling operation, and the tremendous growth of the airline industry during the postwar period turned it into a major corporation. Nonetheless, the Bashful Billionaire didn't have the kind of ready cash that was required to purchase a fleet of jet aircraft, so he sent his agents, their hats in hand, to see the big New York bankers, including David. Also to be visited were the Metropolitan Life Insurance Company, which has a board member who sits on the board of directors of Chase Manhattan Bank, and the Equitable Life Assurance Company, which has four members of its august board on the board of the Chase.

Sure, said the banks and the insurance companies, including Metropolitan and Equitable, they would be happy to lend Howard the several hundred million dollars he needed. On one condition: that if an "adverse development" occurred, Hughes would have ninety days to remedy the situation or lose his voting rights in TWA.

Predictably, an "adverse development" did crop up, and soon Howard Hughes, even though he owned 78.23 percent of the stock in TWA, was forbidden from voting his shareholdings and was ousted from the company's management. In addition, the lenders took over control of TWA's board of directors. The loan Hughes had taken did provide, however, that he could regain control of TWA when he repaid what he borrowed. At that time, presumably, he could vote the bankers and the insurance people off the board of directors.

Howard Hughes was out of his league. He was dealing with the cleverest financial sharks of all time. Soon they had designed a method to get rid of him altogether. Biographer Albert Gerber explained the plan: "Since Hughes Tool Company had supplied airplanes and financing to TWA, it had prevented outsiders from coming in to supply those commodities. This action violated both statutory antitrust laws and the common law duty between the parent and a subsidiary where the subsidiary has minority interest."

Since the lawsuit was filed not by the government, but by TWA, Hughes found himself in the interesting position of being sued by a company in which he owned 78.23 percent of the stock! The New Yorkers demanded complete divestiture of all TWA stock held by Hughes and the Hughes Tool Company.

Hughes had said "I'll never give up TWA," but he was forced to do precisely that. He realized $436,000,000 after taxes from the sale, but the powerful New Yorkers weren't satisfied with just having control of the airline. They continued a suit they had brought against Hughes for alleged mismanagement when he had been in control of TWA (even if he had been guilty, he was mainly mismanaging his own funds), and the courts made Hughes cough up an additional $160,000,000.

David and his pals probably could have broken Hughes altogether, but they chose to show mercy. After all, TWA's prospects had immediately brightened under their management: In 1961 TWA stock was selling for less than $10 a share, but by 1966 it was up to almost $100; the government had awarded TWA new routes; TWA had taken over the Hilton Hotels' international operations; TWA had taken over management of Ethiopian, Saudi-Arabian, and British West Indian Airlines; most important, TWA found credit much easier to come by.

A 1969 Chase Manhattan brochure boasts that their financing helped develop and build the 747 airliners, and that Chase money was helping carriers acquire the new 374-passenger super jets. Actually, Chase had little cause to boast. The bank was simply helping companies they already controlled to get richer. It might have been illegal for Hughes Tool Company to lend money to TWA, but according to the law there is nothing whatever wrong with Chase Manhattan Bank doing the same thing.

David Rockefeller lives an exciting life. He doesn't have to worry about a lack of money hindering what he wants done. Several years ago he assigned an aide to a project, forgot about the matter for a couple months, then called to find out what was causing the delay.

"We underestimated the cost by $50,000," said the aide, "and I'm trying to find a way to make it up."

"Let's not quibble about a few cents," replied David. "Just get the job done."

David's personality could best be described as dull. He doesn't smile often, and if he has a finely developed sense of humor it has eluded his friends, some of whom think the acid-tongued Peggy perfectly complements him.

"I could think of a thousand people to ask to a party," said a wealthy Westchester socialite, "and if David weren't so important he'd be the last person I'd invite. But he is important, and you can't imagine all the politicians and businessmen who'd want to come if they knew he was going to be present."

David is cool, because he can afford to be, and bland, because that is his nature. His face retains a boyish quality, with a look that suggests the denizen of an ivory tower, rather than of a man who has spent most of his adult life in the world's marketplace. David's speech is slow and soft and thoughtful, his words are weighty and professorial. He seldom says "I think" or "I know"; instead he says "One thinks" or "One knows."

David dresses in conservative business suits and straight shirts, wears black shoes and dark socks and quiet ties, has never tried for the sartorial playfulness in which many upper-class men indulge. That would be completely out of character for him. He could, after all, have chosen to while away his life on the Riviera, but instead he goes into the city every morning to work, as others work, as if his livelihood depended on it.

Writer E. J. Kahn, Jr., described the hectic pace David maintains: "Within a forty-eight-hour stretch . . . he went to Cambridge, Massachusetts, to attend commencement exercises at Harvard University, of which he is an overseer; escorted Chancellor Ludwig Erhard of West Germany, to whom Harvard had awarded an honorary degree, back to New York for a dinner held in Erhard's honor by the Council on Foreign Relations, of which Rockefeller is vice president (its executive director, George S. Franklin, Jr., was one of his college roommates and is married to his first cousin); went to Washington the next morning to confer with President Johnson as a member of a businessman's advisory committee on balance of payments; and returned to New York to attend the commencement exercises, that evening, of the Rockefeller Institute, of which he is chairman of the board of trustees."

David is, then, much like the bank he heads, engaged in exciting and important activities, but rather drab when viewed as a separate entity.

Even when he first started at the bank in April, 1946, David was a hard worker. Surely he knew that his name and the force of the family fortune would, by themselves, catapult him to the top, so his industry was commendable; doubly so when it is realized that Junior never worked a day in his life, and that his brothers were hardly knocking themselves out to prove their competitive mettle. Indeed, many people believe it was their lack of industry that galled David, that goaded him to action.

During his early years at the Chase, David made no public pronouncements on the issues of the time, nor did he deliver many speeches. He was in every way the ambitious junior executive, learning the corporate ropes from the bottom up. The day for pronouncements and speeches and decisions that would affect entire nations had not yet arrived.

After he was released from the Army, David moved his family to a red brick Georgian mansion on the 3,500-acre fenced-in enclosure at Pocantico Hills. The mansion and grounds occupy 230 acres, and the broad lawns slope down toward the Hudson. The setting is pastoral. David maintains a stable of riding horses, and sheep and cattle graze on rolling meadows. Peggy busies herself with gardening.

Many upper-class members of society are compulsive purchasers of paintings, and David is no exception. As shown, the paintings can provide a sizable tax write-off, but there is another reason why David, like Junior, has a home that resembles an art gallery: It is a matter of status with the rich.

At David's mansion in Pocantico Hills is a Renoir, an El Greco, a Gilbert Stuart, a Diego Rivera, a Corot, a Bonnard, a Matisse, a Manet, and three Monets. David has paid as much as $200,000 for a painting.

Although David's dress is conservative, his taste in art is definitely avant-garde, and it often clashes with that of his family. Once, to show their displeasure, Peggy and the children assembled a Rube Goldberg statue from tubes, wrenches, pipes, and scrap metal and presented it to David as their own artistic find.

In 1946 David became interested in the Morningside Heights section of Manhattan, a ghetto area in the middle of which stood the Lincoln School, Columbia University, the Union Theological Seminary, the Juilliard School of Music, the Jewish Theological Seminary, and two Rockefeller-endowed institutions, the Riverside Church and International House. David was disturbed at the thought of these cathedrals of culture being surrounded by hordes of the clamoring poor, so he persuaded a number of the institutions to set up an organization called Morningside Heights, Inc., of which he then became president. The aim of Morningside Heights, Inc., was to tear down ten acres of slums and substitute a multimillion-dollar apartment complex for middle-income families. The fact that none of the families presently living in the area could afford the new housing and thus would be uprooted from their homes bothered David not at all. Referring to the area as the "Acropolis of New York," David decided that the apartment complex should be called Morningside Gardens, and he plunged ahead raising federal funds and private investment capital.

But, as E. J. Kahn, Jr., pointed out, bringing Morningside Gardens into being "proved to be not much easier than making the desert bloom. There was, to begin with, the challenging task of getting the trustees of nine nonprofit organizations, not to mention the nine law firms safeguarding them, to agree on any step; beyond that, the sponsors of the venture had to cope with a militant left-wing opposition, called the Save-Our-Homes Committee, which tried to mobilize resistance against the scheme by complaining about a Rockefeller's capriciousness in demolishing the homes of the poor."

This was only the first of many complaints that the left wing would have against David. Later they would level much more serious charges against Junior's youngest, especially when Chase Manhattan Bank went into the international business in earnest and ended up controlling large segments of other countries' economies.

David wasn't prepared for the widespread opposition Morningside Heights, Inc., encountered, and it wasn't until 1954 that the demolition work began (that same year Columbia University gave him an honorary degree, citing him as "relentlessly dedicated"). Finally, in 1957, Morningside Gardens accepted its first tenants.

In April, 1948, David felt his family could use a change of scenery, so he paid $150,000 for the Iselin townhouse at 144–46 East Sixty-Fifth Street, one of the finest residences in Manhattan. David continued to do most of his entertaining at the mansion in Pocantico Hills, but he found the place in New York City more convenient for commuting to and from work. In the backyard of the townhouse, which is four stories high, is a greenhouse that David gave Peggy as a birthday present in 1963.

David also has a home at Seal Harbor, Maine, where for

three weeks each summer he chums around with people like Nathan Pusey, Walter Lippmann, and Thomas Finletter, and another home at St. Bart's in the French West Indies, which he escapes to about twice a year.

Although David wields enormous influence in the corridors of government, he has usually tried to avoid direct political participation. In 1948, however, he did serve as an elector for Thomas E. Dewey.

David is very much involved in politics, and he has reaped considerable criticism for his behind-the-scenes maneuvering, especially where brother Nelson is concerned. In 1960, for example, David was accused of exerting pressure in behalf of Nelson's presidential aspirations on wealthy Republicans who were thinking of donating to the Nixon campaign. If the charges were true, it was a clumsy attempt and it backfired. A number of Nixon supporters, who were also Chase customers, began talking about switching their large corporate accounts to other banks. Nevertheless, if David did try to help his brother politically, he did not try very hard, because, as Ferdinand Lundberg points out, "Every professional politician in the country agrees that if the personable and outgoing Nelson had pressed for the Republican presidential nomination in 1960 he would have obtained it and beaten John Kennedy."

Some people say they see a conspiracy between Nelson and David, with Nelson engineering the passage of laws that make the family richer. When a 1963 bill to amend New York liquor laws was under debate, one Albany legislator pointed out that the statute would make it easier for department stores (many of which are controlled by Chase) to sell whiskey.

David kept pretty much to himself during his first seven years with the bank. Little was written about him, and he said next to nothing for public consumption. As a youngster David was taught what was "appropriate" for an American aristocrat. Now he was being groomed just as carefully in the intricacies of banking, schooled in the conservative practices of big business. When he did emerge in full view in 1953 with a spate of speeches and pronouncements and position papers championing the special interests and privileges of the very rich, it was only after having taken long and exhaustive courses on subjects that no school teaches.

Since 1953 David has never stopped speaking out on what he considers the important issues of the day, and he has become the most listened-to spokesman for Big Business. David is so listened to, in fact, that the *New York Times* devoted almost half a page to covering one of his speeches. Then, in the last sentence, almost as an afterthought, the *Times* added: "Frederick R. Kappel, board chairman of American Telephone and Telegraph, also spoke at the meeting."

I could see the polite features closing down, the firm mouth smiling. It was a discouraging smile.

"Are you sure he won't change his mind?" I asked. "After all, the book will be published whether he talks to me or not."

"I'm afraid the decision is final. As I said, we don't think this book will be in his best interests."

"Who is the 'we' you always talk about?"

Bow Tie raised his hand for silence. "However," he said, "Mr. Rockefeller is a reasonable man. And he is willing to cooperate—to a degree. He said that, if you would put your questions into letter form, he would be happy to answer them."

"I don't want a questionnaire filled out by a committee. I want to see him in person."

"I'm sorry."

"But you're sure he'll answer questions?"

"He said he would."

Chapter VIII

➤➤➤◄◄◄

*I*N MARCH, 1953, David delivered one of his first important public addresses, and the course of action he advocated was a harbinger of things to come. Speaking before the Export Managers Club, David called for the "prompt and drastic reduction of tariffs and trade restrictions by the United States. The removal of tariff barriers is foremost to achieve an expanding economy and a rising standard of living for the free world."

Actually, David wasn't at all concerned with the free world's standard of living. He was concerned with his own. David and his family control three of the seven largest oil companies in the world, including the largest, Standard of New Jersey. The Standard Oil Company of New Jersey makes far more money from foreign oil fields than it does from domestic ones, and it was crystal clear to David that he would rake in even more cash if bothersome tariffs were eliminated.

Some writers, including Harvey O'Connor, contend that the Rockefellers no longer control Jersey Standard, that it is too large. Jersey Standard is indeed large. Two years before David delivered his speech to the Export Managers Club, the *New York Times* (September 13, 1951) reported that Jersey controlled three hundred and twenty-two companies, including Humble Oil and Creole Petroleum, themselves among the largest corporations in the world. Nonetheless, the Rockefellers do control Standard Oil of New Jersey. In 1964, the Rockefeller Brothers Fund owned $61,665,328 worth of stock in the company. Additional large stockholdings are held by the

General Education Board, the Rockefeller Foundation, the Laura Spelman Rockefeller Memorial, Rockefeller Brothers, Inc., and the Chase Manhattan Bank, not to mention the brothers' personal investments in Jersey Standard. Economist Victor Perlo estimates that, if all the chips were on the table, the Rockefellers could produce proxies for almost 65 percent of the company's stock.

Jersey Standard is an unusual company. In fact, it is a corporate marvel. It does not produce, refine, transfer, or sell a single drop of oil. Jersey is a holding company; it merely counts money and plans ways to make more. (The year after David's speech, Creole Petroleum, one of its subsidiaries, raked in $240,000,000 net profit.)

But David wasn't simply interested in Standard Oil of New Jersey when he called for a lowering of tariffs. The Rockefellers also control two other giants of the oil industry, Socony Mobil and Standard of California, plus many other companies dealing in foreign trade. Of course, when these companies need a loan they visit their friend at Chase Manhattan.

The Rockefellers have a sentimental attachment to the companies that formerly comprised the Standard Oil Trust. It was through them that the grandfather made his fortune, and his inheritors are not about to worry about the way he did it. "Standard Oil was a wonderful achievement in its time," David once said, "and we have no reason to apologize for it."

David went on the lecture circuit in earnest in 1953, speaking before business groups, Rotary Clubs, foreign investors, graduating college classes, but it wasn't until March, 1954, that another of his addresses was given nationwide newspaper attention. In his speech, delivered at the University of Chicago's Rockefeller Memorial Chapel, David warned that the nation was headed toward "mass insecurity." A growing trend toward "isolationism," said David, was the largest threat the United States faced, and the way to counter the threat was for business and government to become bolder meeting their overseas responsibilities. David's speech may or may not have been in the best public interest, but it was certainly in his own best interest. Ever since the grandfather cornered the world oil market, much of the Rockefeller fortune has been linked to foreign investment. David wanted protection for those investments, and for the overseas financial expansion he planned, and the safest protection was this country's military might. In addition, the family had invested heavily in defense-oriented businesses, and the success of those enterprises depended on Pentagon spending.

David's interest in international affairs became even more evident in 1954 when he became a charter member of a multination conclave that named itself the Bilderberg. Once each year, cloaked in such secrecy that even the press is excluded, the Bilderberg meets for a long weekend so members can discuss "their views on the state of the world." Prince Bernhard of the Netherlands is chairman of the Bilderberg, and members have included such prestigious people as Hugh Gaitskell, Jean Monnet, Harold Wilson, Dean Acheson, Dean Rusk, Christian Herter, J. William Fulbright, Robert McNamara, George Ball, Henry Heinz II, Henry Ford III, William Moyers, Lester Pearson, Pierre Trudeau, Pierre Mendes-France, Jacob Javits, and Stavros Niarchos. David was host for one of these conferences, held at Williamsburg, Virginia, and he seldom misses a meeting.

An even more important organization that David belongs to—one that has been called, with some justification, "the real United States State Department"—is the Council on Foreign Relations. David has been a director and vice president of the Council on Foreign Relations, and it is difficult to underestimate that organization's influence in shaping U.S. foreign policy.

The Council on Foreign Relations was founded in 1921 but was of little consequence until almost a decade later when it began receiving money from various Rockefeller and Carnegie foundations. CFR membership is restricted to seven hundred resident members (people who have homes or businesses within fifty miles of New York City) and seven hundred nonresident members. The CFR provides a "corporation service," which entails a minimum fee of $1,000 and which provides subscribers with inside information about what is happening within the highest levels of government and finance. Many of America's largest corporations subscribe to this service.

The CFR also provides special studies and reports for the president of the United States, does in-depth research into the economic and political stability of other nations, presents speakers and seminars for subscribers to the corporation service, and publishes the highly influential magazine *Foreign Affairs*.

Members of the CFR regularly shuttle between important posts in industry and important posts in government. CFR members have included Edward R. Stettinius, Paul Cravath, John Foster Dulles, Norman David, John J. McCloy, Arthur H. Dean, Nelson Rockefeller, Allen Dulles, Adlai Stevenson, Lewis Douglas, Thomas Finletter, Devereux Josephs, Walter Lippmann, Myron Taylor, Paul Warburg, and Owen D. Young.

David's influence with CFR is enormous. Many Chase Manhattan Bank directors are active in the organization, and twelve of the twenty trustees of the Rockefeller Foundation are members of the CFR. In addition, David is a trustee of the Carnegie Endowment for International Peace, and eighteen of the twenty-six members of that organization also belong to the CFR.

In 1965 David joined another outfit, the Committee for an Effective and Durable Peace in Asia, to lobby for Lyndon Johnson's war policies in Vietnam. This group, *The Nation* pointed out, "read like a *Who's Who* of the American Establishment," and included such past and present big shots at Chase Manhattan as Eugene R. Black, John J. McCloy, and C. Douglas Dillon.

Taking out large ads in the *New York Times*, this patriotic group proclaimed: "The United States has no territorial ambitions, no desire for bases, no intentions of seeking special privileges or creating spheres of influence anywhere in Southeast Asia."

Leaving aside the ambitions of the United States, David and his friends were hardly so nobly motivated. Chase Manhattan is doing a booming business in most of Southeast Asia, as are several of the Standard Oil companies and the B. F. Goodrich Company, on whose board David sits. It goes without mentioning that much of this business would halt forthwith if the Viet Cong should be successful.

David's fear of nationalization is understandable. He was making money hand over fist with the Punta Alegre Sugar Corporation, an outfit that paid Cubans starvation wages before Castro nationalized it. He was also realizing a nice profit in Peru from the International Petroleum Company, a subsidiary of Standard Oil of New Jersey, until it too was nationalized. The International Petroleum Company, by the way, was a manufacturer of napalm.

The nationalization of International Petroleum Company was a special shock for David. Manuel Prado, who was a son and grandson of former Peruvian presidents, had been an assistant to Nelson Rockefeller during World War II and had also been employed by the Chase. The Rockefellers often have employed relatives or close friends of high government officials. It is a way to assure good will from people in positions of power. It did not work in Peru, however, because the connections Manuel Prado had were with past governments, not the present one.

David's interest in life is not, as some people suspect, solely in the accumulation of money. As mentioned, he is fond of beetles, and in April, 1955, he donated forty-three acres of land in Arizona to the American Museum of Natural History so that organization could study insects and spiders.

The Rockefeller family has never fully accepted the fact that the Chinese people, one-quarter of the human race, no longer purchase their goods and services. Especially for Junior, who regularly visited Standard Oil facilities inside China, the Chinese Revolution was an upsetting experience. Thus it is understandable that, in July, 1955, David urged increased government aid and private investment in India. He feared that the Indian people, despite a number of Rockefeller investments "aimed in part at bettering their lives," might turn to Communism because of pervasive starvation throughout the country. "In this connection," said David, addressing the World Trade Association in San Francisco, "it will be of great importance whether India with Western backing moves faster or slower toward industrialization and higher living standards than China with Russian backing."

India has made little progress alleviating its enormous problems, while China, without Soviet backing, has increased its industrial potential to the point where it can launch satellites into space.

Of course, one of the reasons foreign countries don't benefit as much as they should from David's investments is that he expects to make a profit, a healthy one. This necessarily means that the people doing the actual work in the mines and factories of India are going to have to take what is left over, which is never very much.

To many poor people around the world the name Rockefeller is synonymous with exploitation. David knows this. He also knows that, given the drive of his corporations for profit, U.S. private investment is not likely to better the standard of living of impoverished foreign masses. This is not David's fault. If any blame rests on his shoulders, it is for pretending to believe that a new Standard Oil refinery in some foreign land is going to help the people in that land.

But it is not David's fault. If he paid foreign workers more than he had to, his profits would drop, and powerful as he is he would be replaced, replaced by someone who realizes that a corporation's only business is the making of money. Nonetheless, David is the man at the top, the man who counts the profits of his corporations in the billions, while the men and women who work for his corporations overseas go hungry, and as the man at the top he is an unseen but hated symbol of economic exploitation.

The tragedy is that many of the people going hungry live on

land that is potentially richer than that of the United States. There is more oil in Venezuela than there is in Texas. Jersey Standard's enormous profits in Venezuela are greater than they are in Texas. Yet oil workers in Texas eat quite well, while many in Venezuela literally owe their soul to the company store (usually owned by the same people who own the oil company that pays inadequate wages).

The enormous power David wields is economic. Corporations that he owns span the globe. Most of them make huge profits but, as mentioned, all of the profits come home. They end up in corporate reserves, or in the pockets of stockholders. They do not raise the standard of living of hungry peasants, and for that reason the peasants hate David, and some hate the United States, too, because they believe it is this country's military might that makes David's investments, and their squalor, permanent.

The American Way has been good for David, and he likes to say that free enterprise can make life good for everyone, yet in candid moments he has admitted that no person today could accumulate what he (David) was given. "What Grandfather accomplished was made possible by a unique combination of luck, nerve, and opportunity."

In so many words, David has also admitted that massive private investment overseas primarily benefits the investor: "We cannot be idealistic. Capital must be invested in countries which have the political stability to guarantee a fair deal for businessmen."

Evidently David feels that such a country is China, since he has been in the vanguard urging a reopening of trade with Mao Tse-tung's government. As early as 1955 he was saying it was "political foolishness" to pretend that 700,000,000 people (consumers?) don't exist.

Because companies David controls pay rock-bottom wages ("the going rate," is the way corporate p.r. men put it) does not mean that David is inherently ruthless. If he didn't take advantage of a situation, a competitor would, and stockholders would abandon the Rockefeller companies in droves. David probably doesn't even like what he has to do, but he is faced with economic realities, and he is a realistic man.

David turned his attention away from international matters for a short time in 1956 to "view with alarm the inability of the American people to put aside into savings more than six percent of their income each year." Again, however, David was not concerned with the average citizen's lack of security. His worry, as outlined to the Economics Club of Detroit, was that "saving at this rate probably would be too low to finance the nation's economy."

In other words, huge banks like the Chase would not have as much income at their disposal as they would like, and thus would not be able to make as much money as they would like.

By 1956 David was being hailed by the business community as one of its most important spokesmen. The fact that he was destined to head the powerful Chase Bank in time would have assured that honor anyway, but acquiring respect after only ten years in banking required an additional explanation. A New York City investment banker gave it: "David is saying what the business community wants to hear. He is eloquent, and he has the name, prestige and connections to back up what he says."

David knows where his best interests lie and acts in accordance with those interests. Speaking at Cleveland, Mississippi, in May, 1956, before a group of wealthy businessmen and cotton growers known as the Delta Council, he suggested that what the South needed was an influx of "outside capital to speed a quiet revolution from an agricultural to an industrial economy. The Middle South has an abundance of many of the raw materials for chemicals, among them oil, gas, potash and sulphur."

The "outside capital" David had in mind belonged to the Chase Bank and various corporations the Chase controls, and the idea was that labor costs would be far less expensive in the southern United States.

Five thousand members of the Delta Council listened to

David speak in Cleveland, Mississippi, and they heard him counter their main objection with the following argument: "It is sometimes objected that because interest and dividends go to the investors in the North, the South is paying a form of tribute to that area. In my judgment, this type of thinking does not rest on solid grounds."

Few people could have delivered that statement with a straight face. But David could, and soon the Chase was increasing its loans to southern businessmen. Nor was the Chase refusing interest and dividends, or demanding that southern wages catch up with those in the North.

It is not difficult to see why David champions the causes of the rich. He himself is rich and he pals around with the rich, chats with them, drinks with them, does business with them. Since he has never been a member of the middle or lower class, he does not really relate to or understand their problems. In reality, to expect him to be other than what he is would be asking too much. He exists in a different world than most people. For instance, on the board of directors of the Chase Manhattan Bank are gathered men who directly represent well over one hundred thousand million dollars ($100,000,000,000) in corporate assets. These men are:

Robert O. Anderson, chairman and chief executive officer of Atlantic Richfield Company.

John T. Connor, chairman and chief executive officer of Allied Chemical Corporation.

Ralph Lazarus, chairman of the board of Federated Department Stores, Inc.

C. W. Cook, chairman and chief executive officer of General Foods Corporation.

Joseph A. Martino, honorary chairman of the National Lead Company.

J. Doyle DeWitt, chairman of the Travelers Insurance Companies.

Jeremiah Milbank, Jr., chairman of Commercial Solvents Corporation.

C. Douglas Dillon, chairman of the United States & Foreign Securities Corporation.

Charles F. Myers, Jr., chairman of Burlington Industries, Inc.

William R. Hewlett, president and chief executive officer of Hewlett-Packard Company.

James F. Oates, Jr., director and former chairman of The Equitable Life Assurance Society of the United States.

J. K. Jamieson, chairman and chief executive officer of the Standard Oil Company of New Jersey.

C. Jay Parkinson, chairman and chief executive officer of Anaconda Company.

James A. Perkins, chairman of the Center for Educational Enquiry.

Frederick R. Kappel, retired chairman of the board of American Telephone and Telegraph Company.

Stuart T. Saunders, former chairman and chief executive officer of the Penn Central Company.

Whitney Stone, chairman of Stone & Webster, Inc.

John E. Swearingen, chairman of the Standard Oil Company of Indiana.

Other board members of Chase Manhattan Bank are Herbert P. Patterson, John B. M. Place, George A. Roeder, Jr., Eugene R. Black, George Champion, and J. Richardson Dilworth.

These men, of course, have *indirect* influence over far more than $100,000,000,000, since each sits on approximately four other boards besides the Chase and the company with which they are associated. Indirectly, this influence could run as high as $300,000,000,000.

Protecting and helping to increase the fortunes of the very rich are awesome responsibilities, but David has always found time for leisure. He and Peggy sail a lot, and swim, and play golf, and chase beetles, and they still enjoy a sociable dinner dance.

David and Peggy also enjoy entertaining. At one party David presided over in 1964, there were more than six thousand guests, including Lady Bird Johnson. When asked how he was enjoying the get-together, David replied, "Very much. These are all people I know and like."

Of course, the throwing of large parties leads to the accumulation of large tax deductions, and also provides an informal atmosphere for discussing business deals. "You can learn just so much from routine economic analysis," said one of David's aides. "Around here, in determining what risks we can assume in various parts of the world, we often get our most useful intelligence from David's chats with important people."

What is good for David Rockefeller is not necessarily good for the country. In October, 1956, speaking before an insurance company convention in Chicago, David said that he feared the economy was growing too fast. Unhealthy signs, said David, were record employment, high wages, and near-capacity production!

Morningside Heights, Inc., which David had formed ten years earlier to clear slum housing from an uptown New York area, had accomplished most of its goals by 1956, so David turned his attention downtown, to what one of his aides, Warren Lindquist, called "the heart pump of the capital blood that sustains the free world."

This "heart pump" was, obviously, the Wall Street area, and David formed an organization called the Committee on Lower Manhattan, which soon became the Downtown Lower Manhattan Association. David was chairman of the group, and the idea was to spend $1,000,000,000 of public and private funds for new housing projects, buildings, and parks. David also wanted to relocate the New York Stock Exchange and to construct a pair of hundred-and-ten-story office buildings to house a proposed World Trade Center. To accomplish all this, a number of small businesses would have to be torn down and thousands of low-income families displaced. Had improved housing for the poor and new business sites for the small merchants been provided for, the Downtown Lower Manhattan Association might genuinely have been called public-spirited. Such was not the case, however, nor should anyone have thought it was going to be, after taking a look at some of the people who were on the board of directors of the Downtown Lower Manhattan Association. These included Henry C. Alexander, chairman of the board of J. P. Morgan and Company; James A. McLain, chairman of the Guardian Life Insurance Company; Eugene J. McNeely, executive vice president of the American Telephone and Telegraph Company; William T. Moore, president of Moore-McCormack Lines; Henry S. Morgan, partner in Morgan Stanley and Company; Ralph T. Reed, president of the American Express Company; and Edward C. Shepard, chairman of First National City Bank of New York.

The Downtown Lower Manhattan Association was controversial from the beginning, and for years the concept existed only on an architect's blueprint. Finally, in April, 1964, a serious charge was leveled: bribery. The group David headed paid $10,000 to educational television station WNDT to underwrite the cost of a program entitled "Another Day Downtown." The program was supposed to present both sides of the question of whether a number of stores and housing units should be torn down so a World Trade Center could be constructed, but actually it was a thirty-minute commercial for the views of the Downtown Lower Manhattan Association. People watching the program were not told until it was over that David's group had paid for the show, and even then the amount that had been donated was not revealed. The Downtown West Businessmen's Association, which opposed David's plans because they involved eviction of its members from their stores, charged that the underwriting of the show was an overt bribe to earn the station's good will. All the small businessmen could do, however, was complain, because they didn't have the money to pay for their own program.

Paying for television programs has become common practice. Organizations like the Ford and Rockefeller Foundations, contending that their motivation is altruistic, have given millions to educational TV. Inevitably, the views of these financial giants are carefully adhered to by the stations receiving their largess.

David usually gets his way. The World Trade Center is now well on its way to being completed. The Center will consist of two 110-story towers, the tallest buildings in the world, and will house the governmental and commercial services needed for the smooth functioning of international business.

International business is what David is all about. Speaking before the Arkansas Bankers Association in 1957 at the request of brother Winthrop, David called for the establishment of a Regional Development Authority in the Middle East. The funds for this organization, said David, should come from countries like Iran, Iraq, Kuwait, Qatar, and Saudi Arabia, and among other things the money should be used to widen and deepen the Suez Canal to accommodate the new oil supertankers. In other words, Middle East nations should spend their funds so the Standard Oil companies would find it easier to haul oil away.

David is an avowed Republican, but his influence is strong in both parties. Most knowledgeable politicians believe he could have been John Kennedy's secretary of the treasury had he wanted to be. Columnist William V. Shannon, writing in the *New York Post* several weeks after the 1960 election, said that "President-elect Kennedy would like to have a Rockefeller in his cabinet.

"The prospect is not Governor Rockefeller but his brother David, the head of the Chase Manhattan Bank. He is under serious consideration to be Secretary of the Treasury.

"Kennedy would like to choose a Treasury chief from the business community, but he also wants a business man who is liberal and internationalist. David Rockefeller, a broad-gauged man with an interest in urban renewal and in underdeveloped countries, fits these requirements.

"The only doubtful element is whether David Rockefeller would consider accepting the appointment. . . ."

In 1968 Hubert Humphrey told a *Time* magazine correspondent that he would like to have both David and Nelson Rockefeller in his cabinet, and that if he won the election he would offer them positions. Nelson might have accepted the secretary of state job, but David wouldn't have accepted anything. As *Finance* magazine pointed out, he "has long held the equivalent of a cabinet status in the society of his peers."

Despite Humphrey's admiration for him, David supported Richard Nixon in 1968 because he would be "willing to accept a somewhat higher level of unemployment in order to achieve a greater rate of price stability."

David doesn't need to participate in politics directly to achieve his goals. Many former Rockefeller underlings sit in key government posts, and they seldom recommend policies their former boss wouldn't like. Also, David couldn't possibly do as much inside the government as he can outside. Pointing out that David usually visits the head of state when he visits a foreign country, *Newsweek* said: "Such contacts are beyond the scope of most bank presidents and give the Chase a formidable jump on its competition."

David has had many opportunities to run for public office but has always declined. In 1965 the Republican nomination for mayor of New York City was his for the taking. "The Republican top command," said the *New York Post*, "is seeking a Rockefeller by another name to run for Mayor this November. The Chase Manhattan Bank president, 49, a younger brother of Governor Rockefeller, is a model of the kind of candidate the GOP wants to oppose Wagner."

David easily coexists when Democrats are in power, but he much prefers Republicans. In a speech before the Union League Club in November, 1957, he said that conditions were better for business under Dwight Eisenhower than they could have been under any Democrat. According to David, the Eisenhower Administration created a "whole new atmosphere of confidence because it believed in free enterprise."

Ferdinand Lundberg explained David's confidence in politicians like Dwight Eisenhower: "Presidents McKinley, Theodore Roosevelt, Taft, Wilson, Harding, Coolidge, Hoover and Eisenhower were deep in the confidence of the *finpols* [financial politicians] and, despite harsh words at times purely for public consumption, got along very well with them. Theodore

Roosevelt demagogically referred to them as 'Malefactors of great wealth.' But the *finpols*, always, despite harsh public language, managed to get their way, sooner or later. Corporate concentration, for example, continues apace despite the hullabaloo of antitrust.

"Where the desires of the *finpols* and the government became clearly divergent was in the 1930's, with the country beset by the deep crisis of unemployment initiated by the *finpolities* [powerful corporations]. The formula under which the *finpols* had prospered finally came apart, and government felt the need to improvise. There ensued a period of tension and genuine hostility between *finpols* and government, which was finally poulticed over by the advent of World War II, in which the *finpols* and *finpolities* were very much needed. The fusion of the *finpolities* with the national government, with many *finpols* taken boldly into the national government under the rubric of patriotic effort, was again complete, and was solemnly recemented during the Eisenhower Administration. President Eisenhower frequently expressed his admiration for the *finpols* and gave them a prominent role in his administrations."

David was hardly slowed down by the administrations of John Kennedy and Lyndon Johnson, as Chase Manhattan Bank's skyrocketing assets attest, but there were some unpleasant moments. David publicly attacked Kennedy when the latter rolled back a steel price increase, and did the same with Johnson in the case of aluminum, copper, and steel prices. Despite seeming successes by the presidents, incidentally, it should be pointed out that the big corporations had their way in the long run.

During the 1950s David was not at all reticent about airing his views on important issues, but in 1960, after his promotion to president and chairman of the executive committee of Chase Manhattan Bank, he really broke loose.

"Dear Mr. Rockefeller:

"As you know, I am doing a book about you for Lyle Stuart. One of your aides said you would answer any questions I might have. Here are a few:

"1. Some corporations that you control that do business overseas, notably in South Africa, pay as little as $4.50 a month. Do you think this is a reasonable wage?

"2. You have often come out against full employment in this country. Why?

"3. Do you think $5,000,000 is a fair valuation of the Rockefeller land in Pocantico Hills? Would you sell for that amount?

"4. Do you think there is validity to the assertion, made by an admirer of yours, that you are a self-made man?

"5. As a staunch advocate of individual free enterprise, would you support a law that would limit the amount a person could inherit (to say $50,000)?

"I'll have other questions in a few days. Thanking you in advance, I remain

"Very sincerely yours,
"William Hoffman"

Chapter IX

—»»)«‹‹—

"*B*ANKING operations are so diverse," said the *New Yorker*, "that a very big bank, like the Chase, has a stake in nearly every legislative act."

The Chase also has a stake in the legislative acts of other countries. The bank has offices in the following nations: Austria, Belgium, England, France, West Germany, Greece, Ireland, Italy, Netherlands, Spain, Switzerland, Lebanon, Trucial States, Liberia, Kenya, Malawi, Uganda, Zambia, Botswana, Lesotho, Rhodesia, Swaziland, South Africa, Cameroon, The Gambia, Ghana, Sierra Leone, Nigeria, Bahamas, Dominican Republic, Puerto Rico, Virgin Islands, Barbados, Guyana, Trinidad, Panama, Mexico, Honduras, Argentina, Brazil, Colombia, Peru, Venezuela, Hong Kong, India, Indonesia, Japan, South Korea, Malaysia, Singapore, Thailand, Australia, and South Vietnam.

David's Chase Manhattan Bank has gone international on the grand scale. And it shows no signs of slowing down. Chase Manhattan's 1969 annual report discussed what had been accomplished in that year and what was planned for the future:

"Europe was a major focal point of expansion. New branches were established in Athens and Milan. Plans were advanced for the opening of the bank's fourth and fifth branches in Germany—at Stuttgart and Hamburg—as well as for the construction of a 14-story building in Frankfurt to house the local branch and serve as group headquarters for the growing German branch system.

"The bank also set up a wholly owned subsidiary, Chase Manhattan Bank (Switzerland), in Geneva, and increased its shareholding in the rapidly growing Nederlandsche Credietbank, N.V. in the Netherlands to 25 per cent from $17\frac{1}{2}$ per cent. To cope more efficiently with the burgeoning volume of business in the region, Chase Manhattan opened a new Data Center in London to process the work of several European branches.

"In the Caribbean, Chase Manhattan moved vigorously during the year to expand its activities. The Housing Investment Corporation based in Puerto Rico was acquired early in the year. Chase opened its third branch in Trinidad, at San Fernando, and its sixth in Puerto Rico, at Hato Rey. The latter office is located in a modern 14-story building opened late in 1969 that serves as the bank's headquarters for the Commonwealth of Puerto Rico. A seventh Puerto Rican branch will be opened in 1970, at Carolina. Plans also are proceeding for the opening of nine additional branches in the Caribbean, including the bank's first offices in Barbados [the Barbados office is now in business], Grenada and St. Lucia.

"In South America, Chase Manhattan's associated banks continued their progress and further diversified their activities. In Venezuela, the Banco Mercantil y Agricola, C.A. purchased an interest in the Diners Club of Venezuela. In Brazil, Banco Lar Brasileiro, S.A. acquired a finance company. Moreover, plans are proceeding for the establishment of a new associated bank in Ecuador.

"To increase its capabilities in the Middle East, Chase Manhattan associated with The Commercial Bank of Kuwait S.A.K. and Commerzbank A.G. of Germany to form a new bank, The Commercial Bank of Dubai, LTD., in the Trucial States.

"In the Far East, the bank opened a second branch in Djakarta and entered into an important financial venture in Australia. Chase Manhattan, The National Bank of Australasia and A. C. Goode Associates formed two financial enterprises with a combined capital of $6-million. The joint enterprises are the

Chase-N.B.A. Group, Ltd. and All-States Commercial Bills, Ltd. They will provide medium- and short-term funds, accept deposits and offer a wide range of other financial services in the Australian market.

"Early in 1970, plans were advanced, subject to approval by the Federal Reserve Board, to establish an Edge Act international banking subsidiary headquartered in Los Angeles. This promises to contribute greatly to the bank's expanding overseas activities, particularly throughout the Far East.

"Chase International Investment Corporation (CIIC), a wholly owned subsidiary devoted to financing overseas development projects, enjoyed an active and diversified year. Typical of its new investments, spread over five continents, were a ceramic tile factory in Korea, a fertilizer plant in the Caribbean, a poly-propylene bag complex in Central America and a major printing facility in Argentina."

Chase Manhattan also expanded domestically in 1969, opening five new branches to bring its total to one hundred and fifty-three. During 1969 Chase Manhattan's assets rose $2,800,000,000.

Clearly, David has a large interest in the state of the world, and in 1960, the year he became president and chairman of the executive committee of Chase Manhattan, he greatly increased the number of opinions he offered on how that world could most smoothly function.

Despite his friendship with John Kennedy, David stood firmly in Richard Nixon's corner during the 1960 election campaign. "The economic features of the Democratic platform," said David, "are bound to cause distrust abroad."

In November, 1960, David was honored by the National Committee Against Discrimination in Housing, a group that evidently hadn't studied the way he had had low-income families displaced from Morningside Heights, and how he was lobbying for skyscrapers at the expense of slum dwellers and small businessmen.

David, and especially the Chase Manhattan, has gotten considerable mileage from the fact that the bank has granted loans to set up Negro-owned businesses. The truth is, however, that these loans have been insured by the federal government, and there was no way the Chase could lose money on them.

Less than two weeks after John Kennedy had been elected, David was offering him advice, advice that would later become law. "President-elect Kennedy," said David, speaking before the Cleveland Treasurers Club, "has stated that he favors liberalizing the treatment of depreciation for tax purposes. That may not be enough. As a nation, we may have to face up to the question as to whether a corporate income tax that takes fifty-two percent of all earnings above a certain minimum is consistent with our national objective of a more rapid rate of economic growth."

In January, 1961, David urged the federal government to increase its expenditures for urban renewal. "Just as the tree is doomed to death once the core is rotten," said David, "the city which is healthy only at the fringes cannot long endure." David added: "It is also true that the business community loses important values if the downtown area is allowed to deteriorate."

In 1961 the nation was worried about a continuing deficit in its balance of payments, and David came up with a solution that would not only help the country but also help the Chase. At the Waldorf-Astoria, he outlined his plan to the Economics Club. Here's the way it worked: The government should allow banks to pay higher interest rates and to form special export finance companies that would serve as subsidiaries to provide easy credit for American corporations that wanted to develop products for export.

What had been happening, of course, was that businessmen had been taking advantage of high short-term interest rates offered by foreign banks, and David wanted a piece of the action.

David could have had the Republican nomination for mayor of New York City in 1965, but few people know he could have had it in 1961, too. Senator Keating had recommended him for the job, and a number of politicians had hopes that he would make the race. David was not interested. "Frankly," he told the New York Young Republican Club, "I feel very happy at the Chase Manhattan Bank."

David would have been an interesting political candidate. The large sums of money he could have spent on his campaign would have made him a formidable foe for any opposition. He could have afforded the most knowledgeable strategists, who could have guided him over the shoals of newspaper publicity and televised debates. But David's personality would hardly have excited the voters. Even his closest friends find him somewhat dull, and he is not the sort who would enjoy pressing the flesh. Far from it. Intimates say he has never approved of Nelson's person-to-person campaigning, in which the Governor shovels down pizza and blintzes while the cameras churn and the flashbulbs pop and the crowds mill around shouting, "Hey, Rocky!"

"No one," shudders a Chase vice president, "and I mean no one, calls David Rockefeller, 'Rocky.'"

Most people who have even a nodding acquaintance with tax laws agree that they are weighted in favor of the rich. David disagrees. "The record of the past five years," he told the Columbus, Ohio, Treasurers Club in 1962, "suggests strongly that our tax system bears down too heavily on savings and investment."

Most of David's energies in 1962 were channeled into getting corporate taxes lowered. The *Wall Street Journal*, February 21, 1962, quoted him as saying, "A field where business must exercise leadership is that of tax reform to encourage saving and investment and to provide broader scope for initiative and enterprise. It is clear that the nation suffers from an outmoded tax system which holds back investment and plant modernization to the detriment of all members of our society. Here again, sound policy is often at odds with what is made to have popular appeal from the soapbox."

One of the issues that has popular appeal from the soapbox is the question of whether oil companies should be forced to pay their fair share of taxes. In 1969, the Atlantic Richfield Company, in which David is a major shareholder, avoided paying all but a pittance in taxes on profits that ran into the hundreds of millions of dollars. Atlantic Richfield's good fortune was due in part to the oil depletion allowance, which David has always staunchly defended.

In 1962 *Life* magazine reprinted David's exchange of letters with President Kennedy. David suggested the lowering of corporate taxes, and his suggestion soon became law.

In July, 1962, David appeared before the House Banking and Currency Committee to lobby for his plan to allow banks to pay higher interest rates. Although David was motivated by the knowledge that Chase Manhattan was losing business, what he advocated was sound. When interest payments are lower in this country than they are abroad, short-term capital leaves the United States. Overseas banks then use excess accumulations of dollars to buy gold from the U.S. Treasury Department.

Many people believe that big corporations have grown too powerful. David doesn't see it that way. In a 1962 speech to the American Philosophical Society in Philadelphia, he contended that "the role and influence of business on the American scene has declined relative to that of labor and government."

In 1963 David made one of his more important proposals, the establishment of an International Executive Service Corps, and a year later the project became a reality. Often referred to as the "Executive Peace Corps," the International Executive Service Corps utilizes the skills and experience of retired businessmen to teach managerial and entrepreneurial techniques in foreign countries. The IESC emphasizes assistance to private industries rather than government ones, and a client firm must pay for aid "in order to establish a proper business-to-business relationship."

IESC's sponsors now number more than one hundred and seventy-five multinational corporations. The organization screens requests made by private businesses for professional advice on modern management and industrial techniques, then those companies that are to be helped are shown how to improve and extend a product line and how to obtain loans from development banks.

IESC has had an impressive line-up of chairmen. David headed the group from 1964–68, then was succeeded by George D. Woods, former chairman of the First Boston Corporation and president of the World Bank. Wood's successor as head of IESC was Frank Pace, Jr., chairman of General Dynamics and a former secretary of the Army.

In 1968 alone IESC volunteer executives completed twelve projects in Argentina, three in Venezuela, five in Trinidad, nine in Bolivia, seventy-three in Brazil, twenty in Chile, one in Paraguay, forty-eight in Colombia, sixteen in Costa Rica, two in the Dominican Republic, three in Ecuador, seventy in El Salvador, ten in Guatemala, twenty-two in Honduras, thirteen in Mexico, thirty-one in Nicaragua, forty-two in Panama, and twenty-two in Peru.

In 1965 David became chairman of another group, the Council for Latin America, whose members (over two hundred U.S. corporations) account for more than 80 percent of all U.S. investments south of the border. According to a CLA brochure, the group is the "chief spokesman for U.S. businesses operating in Latin America."

David has an advantage over most people who buy stocks. He and his brothers have more than three hundred "personal" advisers. They also receive a good deal of inside information, from business and government sources alike, that is not available to the common man. However, David is not above giving stock market tips. In a speech delivered to the European Investment Forum in Paris, David recommended that people purchase stocks in "life and risk insurance companies, business equipment companies and companies benefiting from research into drugs."

After delivering his speech to the European Investment

Forum in Paris, David went to London to appear on British television. John Crosby, reporting for the *New York Herald Tribune*, described how most of the interview went:

MODERATOR: Isn't it awful to be rich?

DAVID: No.

MODERATOR: Aren't you miserable being so rich?

DAVID: No.

MODERATOR: Well, isn't it a frightful burden?

DAVID: No, not so bad.

MODERATOR: Aren't there some terrible disadvantages to being so rich?

DAVID: The advantages outweigh the disadvantages.

David seldom appears on television. He has no reason to. Unlike politicians, if he wants something done he does not have to rally public support to do it. Also, TV appearances can prove embarrassing, as he learned when he appeared on the David Frost Show on June 15, 1970.

David appeared on the Frost Show with Prime Minister Olaf Palme of Sweden and Godfrey Cambridge. He and Palme were discussing the relative merits of Sweden and the United States when Cambridge interrupted to say, "One thing I was aware of, having been in Sweden, two or three months ago, was the fact that I never saw a slum while I was there."

David's job was to champion the United States, but, before he had a chance to speak, Palme had said, "We have no present unemployment."

Things went from bad to worse for David. "I was very interested," said Frost, "by the decisions that you and your bodies had to make on the Ralph Nader campaign recently where he was trying to make General Motors responsible by electing three people to the board of directors to make sure that cars were safer and that pollution was limited, and so on. And now Chase Manhattan voted all its shares against Ralph Nader and for General Motors. And Rockefeller University, of which you're chairman, did the same but sent a letter of caution.

Now I wonder which of the two positions you yourself personally feel?"

"I have to make a couple of corrections," David answered. "In the first place, the Chase Manhattan Bank doesn't own and isn't allowed to own any shares itself. It holds shares in a fiduciary capacity for many private people and pension funds. And it votes those shares on behalf of the people who are the beneficiaries. And we voted those shares in favor of management rather than in favor of the Ralph Nader resolution. The reason we did that was that we are acting, as I said, in a fiduciary capacity and we believe that it's in the interest of the shareholders to support management so long as in our judgment management is doing a good job for the company, and hence for their shareholders."

David answered questions about tipping in restaurants (he's not a big tipper), about what he likes to receive for Christmas (wine), and about whether he was happy (yes), and then it was almost time to sign off, so Frost asked if he had any advice to pass on to the viewers. David related a story from Junior, who in turn had gotten it from the Horse's Mouth, about how opportunity and responsibility go hand in hand. David was drawing breath to say more when the free enterprise system cut him off for the final fade-out and a flurry of commercials.

David seldom loses his cool but he did, once, on October 7, 1963. It occurred during a speech he was giving in Washington, D.C., and it was the result of what David considered a long series of anti-Chase Manhattan decisions by the federal government. The *New York Herald Tribune*'s national economics editor, Joseph R. Slevin, described the action: "Chase Manhattan Bank president David Rockefeller delivered a blistering attack against the Controller of the Currency, James J. Saxon, yesterday, but the combative Federal official gave the New Yorker a polite brushoff.

"Mr. Rockefeller told Mr. Saxon that 'he would be well advised to show greater restraint in exercising the immense power he now possesses.' He warned that the controller may destroy the dual banking system and charges that his policies have produced embarrassment and confusion.

"The powerful but normally restrained banker blasted Mr. Saxon at the opening session of the American Bankers Association convention. Chase Manhattan is a state-chartered bank, and Mr. Rockefeller addressed the ABA's state bank division.

"Mr. Saxon got his chance to reply at the National Bank division meeting yesterday afternoon. He drew laughter and applause in Constitution Hall by suggesting that some delegates had taken off their coats because of the 'heat'—then read through a prepared speech before again alluding to the Rockefeller criticisms."

David is a powerful man, much more powerful than James J. Saxon, probably even more powerful than the men behind Saxon who had precipitated the dispute, but for the moment he had been frustrated and had vented that frustration with angry words. Eventually, David seems certain to get what he wants.

What David wanted in 1963 was a blank check for Chase Manhattan to move into the suburbs and upstate New York by means of branches and mergers. Previously David had been blocked by a state law which confined the Chase to the five boroughs of New York City, but brother Nelson had taken care of that in 1960 with a bill that permitted the big city banks to expand. Chase and First National City (controlled by another branch of the Rockefeller family) jumped at the opportunity, and that's when Controller of the Currency James J. Saxon entered the picture. Saxon wisely recognized that huge banks like Chase Manhattan would soon swallow all competition, that big as they were, they would become even bigger. Saxon ruled that, if city banks wanted to go into the suburbs, they would have to build branches of their own.

This made David angry. He had planned the expansion of the Chase to take place through mergers. It would be easy, fast, inexpensive. Saxon, backed by a powerful small-bank lobby in Congress, said no.

To this day, except for enormous overseas expansion, Chase

Manhattan Bank has pretty much remained in New York City. But how much longer will it go on? How much longer can people like James Saxon and the small bankers stand in the way of the Chase juggernaut? Despite evidence to the contrary, can the "little" man really survive?

Chase Manhattan Bank's assets have more than doubled in the last decade. They now exceed $23,000,000,000. The Chase makes more loans to large businesses than any other bank. The Chase, through its trust departments, controls more major corporations than any other institution. The Chase is the most powerful financial corporation in this country; in fact, it is the most powerful financial corporation in the world. The chairman of the Chase, bland, soft-spoken, dull as he is, probably wields more influence than any other man on earth.

In 1970, could someone like James J. Saxon again stand up to David and say no?

"Dear Mr. Rockefeller:

"I imagine that you have not yet had time to answer my first letter. I'd like you to know that the book is coming along quite well and that many of your aides, and even some of your relatives, have been most cooperative. I still have a few questions, however, that I believe you are best qualified to answer.

"1. Why does your bank take credit for making loans to black businessmen when in reality the repayment is guaranteed by the federal government?

"2. Do you think that the existence of great wealth (yours) and great poverty (slum dwellers) within a few miles of each other is morally justifiable?

"3. If it is not morally justifiable, do you intend to give away what you have and to strike out on your own?

"4. If, as you said, the Vietnam War is 'a burden we must be prepared to shoulder in defense of freedom,' do you consider the astronomical rise in your bank's profits in the past five years an example of that burden?

"5. My last question is a personal one. I have fifty dollars to play around with and wonder if you would recommend a stock?

"I look forward to receiving your answers, and I will send you an autographed copy of the book when it is finished.

                                        "Sincerely Yours,
                                        "William Hoffman"

Chapter X

❯❯❯〉〈❮❮❮

*C*HASE Manhattan Bank's assets grew enormously during the second half of the 1960s. But with its increasing power came increasing criticism, from a variety of sources.

David's most consistent critic was Representative Wright Patman of Texas, head of the House Banking and Currency Committee. In July, 1967, Patman delivered a broadside against several of the Rockefellers, but such is the power of Junior's sons that they could shrug and say, "No comment," when asked by the press to reply.

Patman began his attack by accusing Nelson of running New York State by "trickery, slickery, shell games, gambling and fast-buckism." Patman said that New York desperately needed tax revenue, but that instead of getting it where he should—from the profits of huge tax-exempt foundations—Nelson had initiated a lottery "that would hurt the lunch pailers" while not "disturbing the peace of mind or the peace of pocket of his cronies in the swank social clubs of New York.

"I intend to show," said Patman, "that this is simply another Rockefeller scheme to dodge a fair and equitable tax program. New York State would be rolling in tax money if tax-exempt foundations were subject to levies, but this won't happen because the history of the Rockefeller family is one of tax-dodging, not tax-paying."

Patman also charged that the New York Lottery was not only a way the Rockefellers could save money, but that it was a way they could make money. And, indeed, Chase Manhattan's many branches were given a franchise to sell lottery tickets and, of course, to receive a commission from their sale.

Wright Patman wasn't the only person who did not like the way the Chase was operating. David had found a means to stem the flow of exodus dollars to higher-interest-paying foreign banks, and William McChesney Martin, Jr., chairman of the Federal Reserve Board, called the method "particularly inappropriate at the present time, when a restrictive monetary policy is in effect."

What David was doing was urging large depositors to put their money in Chase Manhattan's Virgin Islands branches, branches that were not subject to the Federal Reserve Board's prohibition against paying more than $6\frac{1}{4}$ percent interest on deposits of $100,000 or more.

David originally had contended that his desire to pay higher interest rates was patriotically motivated, that it was a way to stop the gold outflow. However, the government's balance-of-payments program, which put innumerable restrictions on who could deposit money in foreign banks, had begun to alleviate the problem when David showed what his real interest was: increasing the money Chase Manhattan had on deposit. Although the Virgin Islands are considered part of the United States, they were not subject to government regulations concerning interest rates and balance of payments. Thus David could pay whatever interest he wanted to and not violate any laws. The *New York Times* said that David was taking advantage of "a gaping loophole in the Federal Reserve's regulations," and William McChesney Martin called it "dangerous," but, rather than pulling back, David went forward. He not only continued telling people to put money into Chase's Virgin Island branches, but began urging depositors to put money in Puerto Rican branches of the Chase as well.

In January, 1968, David outlined his "do-it-yourself" philosophy on how blacks and Puerto Ricans could get ahead in business. David spent a good deal of time deploring the fact that disadvantaged people "have managed to get high school diplomas with no more than fifth-grade reading ability," that they "have only the vaguest notion of what constitutes punctuality and proper attire," and that they suffer "from an almost total lack of motivation." David made these observations to the Federal Equal Employment Commission, but he had nothing to say about the testimony before the same group of Ralph H. Skinner, an Eastern Airlines vice president. Skinner acknowledged that Eastern employed only one black pilot out of eight hundred and sixteen, and that the first black stewardess hadn't been hired until 1965.

Chase Manhattan Bank, it should be noted, has the minority controlling interest in Eastern Airlines.

During David's testimony, he was asked by commission member Daniel Steiner whether Chase Manhattan could use its prestige to assist in getting blacks hired by brokerage houses. "I think example is the most important way to influence people," said David. "It will not help to go around preaching. Being self-righteous will not help."

David has not been in the forefront of the civil rights struggle. When the late Whitney Young, executive director of the National Urban League, said that David Rockefeller, Henry Ford, and George Meany should lead a march of whites on Washington to demand that Congress put top priority on racial and urban problems, David said it would be "inappropriate."

The *New York Herald Tribune*, August 1, 1964, summarized in one paragraph the purpose of one of David's visits overseas: "The world's foremost Communist, Soviet Premier Nikita Khrushchev, and one of its leading capitalists, David Rockefeller, met for two hours and fifteen minutes yesterday. Naturally, they talked about money."

After talking with Khrushchev, David went to Paris and discussed the possibilities of increasing East-West trade. "The Soviets must meet certain minimum expectations," he told an international conclave of businessmen, "in terms of the protection of legal rights, the payment of debts, freedom from bureaucratic delays and interference and the creation of an overall climate conducive to greater confidence before we can consider liberalizing our trade with them. However, if we see evidence of good faith on these scores, then I am persuaded that we should look seriously for ways of increasing East-West trade."

When David returned to the United States, he met with Lyndon Johnson to tell him what had happened during the talk with Khrushchev, but it wasn't until later that the full significance of the Russian visit emerged.

In 1967 the International Basic Economy Corporation, owned by David and his brothers, announced that it was entering the Soviet Union and other eastern European countries in a multibillion-dollar operation. Joining fifty-fifty with Tower International, Inc., which is controlled by Cyrus Eaton, IBEC was to build, or to complete already begun, large hotels in Bucharest, Sofia, Budapest, Belgrade, Prague, and Warsaw. IBEC and Tower International were also to build two hundred million dollars' worth of rubber plants in the Soviet Union, a fifty-million-dollar aluminum plant in Yugoslavia, and a glass plant in Rumania.

In November, 1964, speaking at Brown University, Junior's alma mater, David suggested the establishment of a clearing house that would correlate and distribute to universities the voluminous flow of special reports and periodic publications put out by big business. "Hundreds of companies," said David, "issue thousands of reports annually that span the spectrum of industry, commerce, and finance. These publications project trends in worldwide trade, in international investment, in consumer spending, in governmental expenditures, in product development, manufacturing, and marketing."

David suggested that Brown University might have sufficient space to start such a program. What he didn't say was that the plan would benefit big business a great deal more than it would benefit Brown University students.

Another facet of David's personality emerged on January 8, 1965, during a talk with a *New York Post* reporter. "One really is upset," said David, "when people feel that because one has money it makes differences in your personality or the way you deal with people."

In a speech delivered at Columbia University's Graduate School of Business in April, 1964, David unveiled a plan "to encourage business investment and spur economic growth." He suggested that Congress give up (to an "executive committee") some of its constitutional authority to raise and lower taxes. The executive committee, said David, would be able to move much faster during "times of emergency" to grant "depreciation allowances and investment credits."

David does indeed champion the interests of his class, most of whom are Republicans. Unfortunately, this causes David to embrace positions that are not substantiated by fact. When the *New York Times* criticized House Republicans for voting to cut back foreign aid, David was moved to write the newspaper a letter. Here's part of what he wrote: "While there were many Republicans among those who voted against foreign aid, the record is by no means as one-sided as you indicated. In the Foreign Affairs Committee a substantial majority of the Republican members voted to support Chairman Thomas E. Morgan in reporting out a very good bill. These same Republican committee members, led by Peter Frelinghuysen of New Jersey, also gave the legislation strong support on the floor."

Despite David's defense of Republicans, however, the truth is that they voted 153 to 23 to recommit the foreign aid bill, and that all but one of the successful floor fights to cut funds was led by a member of the GOP.

It is difficult, in a way, to understand David's unwavering adherence to Republican Party principles. The Democrats have never made life difficult for the Rockefellers. In fact, the Democrats were in power during World War I, World War II, the Korean War, and the Vietnam War, each of which were conflicts the family wholeheartedly supported and made great sums of money from. In addition, it was a Democrat (Johnson) who had corporate taxes lowered and a Democrat (Truman) who initiated the Marshall Plan, which enabled the Rockefellers to make millions.

In June, 1966, David was elected president of the Harvard Board of Overseers. He succeeded Neil H. McElroy, former secretary of defense, as head of America's oldest university governing body. Actually, David had been a member of the Board of Overseers since 1954, when he had been only thirty-nine years old.

David was given another award by Harvard in 1961, at a twenty-fifth class reunion, when he was chosen as the outstanding graduate of 1936. This was a signal honor for a man whose only academic distinction in four undergraduate years was an "A" in a course taught by an ant specialist.

David is mild-mannered and soft-spoken and polite. He likes to carry other people's suitcases. He is never rude. David hardly seems the sort to stir up controversy. But he does, because his business is controversial, as are his proposals. However, few of his proposals were greeted with the cynicism and open hostility accorded the one he made to the Canadian Club in February, 1967. On that occasion David suggested that the United States and Canada form their own Common Market. "Those who deny the feasibility or desirability of free trade between the United States and Canada," said David, "overlook the degree to which trade between the two countries is already free. In dollar value, more than half the goods which cross the border do so without paying duty."

David's suggestion was not one the Canadians took kindly. United States capital already dominated much of Canada's economy, and the abolition of trade barriers might have made the domination complete. It would have been difficult for smaller, less wealthy Canadian firms to compete with this country's super-corporations.

David thinks in large terms. At the same time he suggested the Common Market for Canada and the United States, he said: "In time Mexico could join, and even Great Britain if its attempts to enter the European Common Market fail."

Britain and Mexico were no more enthusiastic about the idea than Canada was.

Later in 1967, in May, David also made himself unpopular with certain residents of San Francisco. It was then that he made public his plans for a $150,000,000 building project to be called the Embarcadero Center. David and his brother Winthrop were partners in the deal, which called for construction near the San Francisco waterfront. Unfortunately, David's plans clashed with local building codes, which for scenic purposes outlawed any structure more than twenty-five stories high. Plans for the Embarcadero Center, which San Franciscans renamed Rockefeller Center West, called for a sixty-story office building and a forty-five-story office building. Prominent architects and planning experts criticized the project, which also was to have a twenty-five-story, two-block-long office building, a sixteen-story hotel, three theaters, shops, restaurants, and a wine museum and a wine library. David appeared before the city-county Board of Supervisors, emphasizing that the Embarcadero Center's "outdoor areas would be graced with more than one million dollars' worth of sculpture and other art works" and that half of the area would be open space.

David won. Local financial interests and spokesmen for organized labor backed his plans, and city-county politicians rewrote the building codes.

David usually wins. He accomplishes things the ordinary citizen couldn't even attempt. The reason is m-o-n-e-y, that marvelous green stuff that speaks a universal language. It is David's calling card, his passkey. People do David's bidding not because of his personality or his wit, but because of his money and the sheer power of it.

In June, 1967, David delivered a speech that surprised a large number of antiwar dissidents. The occasion was the commencement exercise for the Choate School, from which his son Richard was being graduated, and David began his address by saying: "Even responsible dissent may not be a welcome element on every occasion, but the first point I want to make is that it is absolutely essential to progress. Without the change bred by honest and enlightened dissent, man is bound to die in mind, spirit, and body. It is his unique ability to be dissatisfied that imbues him with the dedication and drive required for the enlightenment of all great works."

Questioners and dissenters, David went on to say, have made "most of the social and scientific breakthroughs in history. Thomas Edison once said, 'Show me a satisfied man and I will show you a failure.' "

David's liberal views on dissent soured somewhat as opposition to the Vietnam War increased. In 1969, prior to a planned demonstration at the induction center on Whitehall Street, only a stone's throw from Wall Street, David telephoned Mayor Lindsay and demanded that the entire financial district be walled off. Bank windows had been broken in the past and David wanted no more of it. Worse, Chase Manhattan Bank Plaza had been bombed several times, presumably by people unhappy with Chase's financial success during a period of war, and this clearly was not the type of dissent he had advocated at the Choate School.

In November, 1970, David decided to try his luck on television again. The program was "Banks and the Poor," sponsored by National Educational Television, and David found himself debating his old nemesis, Representative Wright Patman of Texas. Here is an exchange between David and Representative Patman:

DAVID: The Chase Manhattan Bank has been very glad to be one of eighty banks which have participated in a mortgage pool designed to improve the housing conditions and opportunities for people in the Bedford-Stuyvesant section of Brooklyn, which of course is the black concentrated area of Brooklyn. I think unquestionably this project was a highly desirable one. I'm bound to say that like some other projects with high ideals and objectives, it was a little slow in getting off the ground. It hasn't generated the amount of interest that its sponsors hoped that it would. We have invested, we've committed to invest up to five million dollars; of that only seven hundred thousand has actually gone out. We have, however, through our real estate and mortgage department, given a good deal of assistance to the program and we're hopeful that it is going to move faster in the future. We're eager to put the money out if the opportunities present themselves.

PATMAN: Now the second largest bank in the world is the Chase Manhattan Bank, and David Rockefeller is the head of that bank. He testified before my committee on banking and currency, soon after that rate of interest was increased from $7\frac{1}{2}$ percent to $8\frac{1}{2}$ percent. We were trying to determine why that was done, and we wanted to find out where the money was going. We found out that very little of the money was going for housing, very little. In the Chase Manhattan Bank, as big as it is, worth fifteen or twenty billion dollars, they were only putting a few million dollars in housing, just a very few, a very insignificant amount, but in gambling casinos like the Resort International which Chase Manhattan bought a substantial interest in, about that time, you know they had plenty of money to go into Resort International which operates for a profit. They had plenty of money to go into that. They have had plenty of money for speculation. They have had plenty of money for everything, except one of the essentials of family life—adequate shelter. They didn't have any money for that.

DAVID: Congressman Patman is a very distinguished and successful politician. I think his prejudices and biases in the banking industry are quite well known. I understand that when he was a young man, he was once turned down for some loan that he tried to make in his local Texas bank, and he seems to have taken a rather dim view of bankers ever since.

PATMAN: My concern about the abuses of the large commercial banks does not stem from any personal disappointment, as claimed by Mr. Rockefeller. This is an old story that has been falsely disseminated by the highly paid banking lobbies here in Washington and all over the country. I have never been turned down by any bank or banker for a loan and there has never been any unpleasantness between me or any bank or banker. Big bankers like Mr. Rockefeller simply aren't used to being challenged, and when someone questions their activities, they feel they have to find some excuse. The fiction about Wright Patman isn't the issue. The issue is what the big banks are doing against low-income Americans.

"Banks and the Poor" revealed one of the reasons that the big banks usually get their way with Congress. Although House Rule 8 says that, where the private interests of a member are concerned in a bill or question, he is to withdraw, the following congressmen, all with bank holdings or serving as bank directors, have disregarded House Rule 8 and taken part in the vote on recent major banking legislation:

Watkins M. Abbitt (D.-Va.); John M. Ashbrook (R.-Ohio); J. Glenn Beall, Jr. (R.-Md.); William G. Bray (R.-Ind.); Jack Brooks (D.-Tex.); George E. Brown, Jr. (D.-Cal.); James T. Broyhill (R.-N.C.); Joel T. Broyhill (R.-Va.); Omar Burleson (D.-Tex.); John N. Happy Camp (R.-Okla.); Bob Casey (D.-Tex.); Tim Lee Carter (R.-Ky.); William V. Chappell (D.-Fla.); James C. Cleveland (R.-N.H.); Harold R. Collier (R.-Ill.); William M. Colmer (D.-Miss.); Glenn R. Davis (R.-Wis.); James J. Delaney (D.-N.Y.); John R. Dellenback (R.-Ore.); David W. Dennis (R.-Ind.); Edward J. Derwinski (R.-Ill.); Harold D. Donohue (D.-Mass.); Thomas N. Downing (D.-Va.); John J. Duncan (R.-Tenn.); Frank E. Evans (D.-Colo.); George H. Fallon (D.-Md.); Leonard Farbstein (D.-N.Y.); Dante B. Fascell (D.-Fla.); Michael A. Feighan (D.-Ohio); Peter H. B. Frelinghuysen (R.-N.J.); Samuel N. Friedel (D.-Md.); Cornelius E. Gallagher (D.-N.J.); Robert N. Giaimo (D.-Conn.); Sam M. Gibbons (D.-Fla.); James R. Grover (R.-N.Y.); Durward G. Hall (R.-Mo.); John Paul Hammerschmidt (R.-Ark.); Wayne L. Hays (D.-Ohio); F. Edward Hebert (D.-La.); Lawrence J. Hogan (R.-Md.); Chet Holifield (D.-Cal.); Craig Hosmer (R.-Cal.); James J. Howard (D.-N.J.); Edward R. Hutchinson (R.-Mich.); Richard H. Ichord (D.-Mo.); John Jarman (D.-Okla.);

Harold T. Johnson (D.-Cal.); Charles Raper Jonas (R.-N.C.); Robert E. Jones (D.-Ala.); Tom Kleppe (R.-N.D.); Alton Lennon (D.-N.C.); William M. McCulloch (R.-Ohio); Robert C. McEwen (R.-N.Y.); William S. Mailliard (R.-Cal.); Robert B. Mathias (R.-Cal.); John Melcher (D.-Mont.); George P. Miller (D.-Cal.); William E. Minshall (R.-Ohio); Chester L. Mize (R.-Kan.); Robert H. Mollohan (D.-W.Va.); G. V. Montgomery (D.-Miss.); William S. Moorhead (D.-Pa.); Thomas E. Morgan (D.-Pa.); John E. Moss (D.-Cal.); John T. Myers (R.-Ind.); William H. Natcher (D.-Ky.); Thomas P. O'Neill, Jr. (D.-Mass.); Otto E. Passman (D.-La.); Claude Pepper (D.-Fla.); Carl D. Perkins (D.-Ky.); J. J. Pickle (D.-Tex.); Otis G. Pike (D.-N.Y.); Richard H. Poff (R.-Va.); Melvin Price (D.-Ill.); James H. Quillen (R.-Tenn.); Thomas M. Rees (D.-Cal.); Henry S. Reuss (D.-Wis.); John J. Rhodes (R.-Ariz.); Ray Roberts (D.-Tex.); Byron G. Rogers (D.-Colo.); Paul G. Rogers (D.-Fla.); Dan Rostenkowski (D.-Ill.); Edward R. Roybal (D.-Cal.); Phillip E. Ruppe (R.-Mich.); John P. Saylor (R.-Pa.); Herman T. Schneebeli (R.-Pa.); Joe Skubitz (R.-Kan.); Henry P. Smith III (R.-N.Y.); Robert T. Stafford (R.-Vt.); William J. Stanton (R.-Ohio); Robert G. Stephens, Jr. (D.-Ga.); Leonor K. Sullivan (D.-Mo.); Roy D. Taylor (D.-N.C.); Morris K. Udall (D.-Ariz.); John C. Watts (D.-Ky.); J. Irving Whalley (R.-Pa.); John W. Wydler (R.-N.Y.); and Larry Winn, Jr. (R.-Kan.).

Clearly David has little to fear from the United States House of Representatives.

The fourth quarter of 1966 was the most profitable in Chase Manhattan Bank's history, but the record lasted only until the third quarter of 1967. During the latter period Chase Manhattan's profit margin (net operating earnings as a percentage of its gross operating revenues) was 16.2 percent. In the third quarter of 1967 Chase paid out $209,000,000 in interest and collected $376,000,000.

David went overseas in October, 1967, to tell the English that it was "good for Britain to have more American capital here." David was responding to Prime Minister Harold Wilson's warning that continued United States economic domination could lead to "industrial helotry, in which we would be put on a par with the serfs of ancient Sparta."

David was calling for an increase in taxes to support the Vietnam War long before Lyndon Johnson had the surtax enacted into law. He also called for an extension of the surtax after its initial run. "Unless the government acts by diverting purchasing power from its citizens," David told the American Newspaper Publishers Association in April, 1968, "it will do so by inflation, in President Johnson's words, 'the cruelest tax of all.'"

David was using the age-old argument of the very rich, that the way to keep prices in line is to decrease the common man's purchasing power. It is interesting to note that big businessmen never call for restraint on their own part, such as taking less profit while their employees narrow the earnings gap. If prices are to be maintained or brought down, the first to suffer must be the consumer. He must be laid off, or taxed to decrease his buying power, or charged higher interest to discourage borrowing. Swollen corporate earnings or reserves must not be tapped to fight inflation.

In July, 1968, a House Banking subcommittee headed by Wright Patman issued a report saying that banks (as trustees for pension funds), foundations, private trusts, and actual owners exercise influence (much of it voting influence) over corporate assets totaling $607,000,000,000, and 34.5 percent of this total was concentrated in New York State banks. The Patman Report went on to say that, among the companies whose stock was held in large amounts by bank-trust departments, were "18 companies publishing 31 newspapers and 17 magazines, as well as operating 17 radio and TV stations. Among the more prominent are Time, Inc., Newsday, Inc., The Evening News Association (Detroit), Booth Newspapers, Inc., The Tribune Company (Chicago), The Copley Press, Inc., The Hartford Courant Company, A. S. Abell Company (Baltimore Sun Papers), and The Dow Jones Company."

The Patman Report revealed that Chase Manhattan Bank controlled 5.9 percent of the stock in the Columbia Broadcasting System, and that it had interlocking directorships with The New York Times Company and the American Broadcasting Company.

FOUNDATION	ASSETS, EARLIEST DATE AVAILABLE	ASSETS, LATEST DATE AVAILABLE
American Association for Economic and Social Development	$ 20,000	$ 413,865
China Medical Board	$21,258,515	$ 56,538,632
Colonial Williamsburg	$ 248,766	$ 109,222,086
Agricultural Development Council	$ 58,160	$ 6,338,187
Esso Education Foundation	$ 1,452,146	$ 5,784,367
Government Affairs Foundation	$ 131,851	$ 29,820
Rockefeller Brothers Fund	$ 164,635	$ 190,967,245
Rockefeller Foundation	$35,965,384	$ 736,222,598
Rockefeller Institute	$ 8,686,345	$ 249,182,875
Sealantic Fund	$ 3,787	$ 9,368,160
Sleepy Hollow Restorations	$ 1,962,977	$ 20,937,722
Standard Oil (Indiana) Foundation	Unknown	$ 44,927,493
Rockwin Fund	Unknown	$ 30,676
TOTALS	$69,952,566	$1,429,963,726

One controversial practice Chase Manhattan engages in is that of "marriage broker" (in business parlance a corporation that brings two or more other corporations together for the purpose of merger). The Chase wants to see its customers grow so they will have greater need for bank services and more money to keep on deposit. The Chase also receives a fee when a merger is consummated, another reason for the fact that the bank maintains a list of almost two thousand companies that are eager either to acquire or sell. What the New York Stock Exchange didn't like was that proposed mergers were often kept secret until the last moment, which meant that people like David could buy stock with the absolute assurance that it was going up. In 1968 the New York Stock Exchange tightened its disclosure policy, but not enough to deny corporate insiders a big jump on other investors.

Things were nothing but rosy for the Chase Manhattan Bank during 1968. Earnings reached an all-time high. At the end of the year, David's salary was increased to $253,000, but that was peanuts compared to the dividends he was receiving.

The year 1969 was even better for Chase. The inflation that ate away the paychecks of most Americans affected David's colossus not at all. In May the bank paid a whopping 50-percent stock dividend.

In the fall of 1969, David took an extended tour of the Middle East, visiting Israeli and Arab leaders alike. At the end of his visit he reported his observations to President Nixon.

David and his brothers exert *indirect* influence over hundreds of billions of dollars. But their *direct* influence should not be sneered at either. A March 26, 1968, Wright Patman subcommittee report titled "Tax Exempt Foundations and Charitable Trusts: Their Impact on Our Economy," revealed Rockefeller Foundation holdings as shown on page 165.

In almost every instance, the Rockefellers maintain control of how this money is used, and how the foundations vote their shareholdings.

In 1937 the Temporary National Economic Committee (TNEC) issued a report showing what each of the twenty largest stockholders held in major industrial corporations. Ferdinand Lundberg, using the TNEC study, computed the worth of Rockefeller holdings at 1964 closing prices (page 167).

Even these figures fail to give a true picture of how much the Rockefellers directly control. The TNEC study was limited to the twenty largest stockholders in a given corporation. Lesser stockholdings were not listed. In addition, TNEC confined itself to industrial companies so the Chase Bank was

COMPANY (name used in 1937)	1964 PRICES
Atlantic Refining Company	$ 6,821,025
Bethlehem Steel Corporation	$ 10,379,268
Consolidated Edison	$ 10,170,255
Consolidated Oil Corporation	$ 49,058,436
Continental Oil Company	$ 14,055,174
Illinois Central Railroad	$ 536,364
International Harvester Company	$ 24,604,360
Middle West Corporation	$ 8,272,495
Missouri-Kansas-Texas Railroad	$ 115,679
Norfolk and Western Railway	$ 782,073
Ohio Oil Company	$ 190,165,807
Pere Marquette Railway	$ 23,927
Phelps Dodge Corporation	$ 5,381,811
Radio Corporation	$ 4,362,775
Santa Fe Railway	$ 1,576,563
Socony Vacuum Oil Company	$ 771,303,099
Standard Oil Company of California	$ 664,330,693
Standard Oil Company of Indiana	$ 334,335,677
Standard Oil Company of New Jersey	$2,628,070,253
U.S. Steel Corporation	$ 3,361,473
Western Pacific Railroad	$ 3,916,487
TOTAL	$4,741,515,014

not included, nor were Rockefeller Center and a host of real estate and insurance holdings. As Professor Lundberg pointed out, "If a man were to own whatever the Rockefellers, Du-Ponts or Mellons held that was not even counted in the TNEC study, he would be one of the nation's nabobs."

David and his brothers are wealthy beyond most people's wildest dreams, and to acquire their money required nothing more strenuous than listening to a will being read, or signing their names to dividend and trust account checks. There are persons who resent the Rockefellers because they themselves were not so fortunate. But there are other persons who resent the Rockefellers for more valid reasons.

It had been three months since my second letter to David Rockefeller, and the book was almost finished. Three months, and no answer. I really hadn't expected one. What, after all, could he say?

I had come to realize that things either make sense, moneywise, or they don't. What if David was rich and hadn't earned it? What if he was powerful simply because of his name? So what?

I called the bank. After a long wait on the *Hold* button, I was talking with Bow Tie again. I asked him why I hadn't heard from David.

"Mr. Rockefeller has been out of town," was the answer.

"For three months?" I asked.

There was a brief flutter of laughter to concede the point, then, "It almost seems that way. He hardly sits down before he's off again. And not on some pleasure trip, either. I hope you're making that clear in your article—er, book."

"Yes," I said, "I'm sure he's plugging away."

Chapter XI

→»×«←

SOUTH Africa is a lovely country of sparkling water and great vistas of land. It lies under a huge blue sky that has not yet been sullied by smoke and soot.

South Africa is a rich country. It has a vast wealth of natural resources, including gold and diamonds and oil, and the 3.7 million whites who live there enjoy the fourth highest standard of living in the world. Unfortunately, the 12 million blacks who live there do not.

The system is called apartheid, and it is supported not only by the government and the white population, but by the Dutch Reform Church, which justifies it on the grounds that it preserves Christian and European culture.

In the past twenty-five years the annual wage for blacks has dropped from $203 to $196. But as early as 1897 wages were being cut. Here's the way George Albu, Chairman of the Association of Mines, justified one pay decrease during testimony before a Commission of Inquiry in Johannesburg: "The Native at the present moment receives a wage far in excess of the exigencies of his existence. The Native earns between fifty shillings ($12.15) and sixty shillings ($14.58) a month, and he pays nothing for food and lodging. In fact, he can save almost the whole amount he receives . . . if he can save twenty pounds ($97.20) a year it is almost sufficient for him to go home and live on the fat of his land. In five or six years the native population will have saved enough money to make it unnecessary for them to work any more. The consequence will be most disastrous for the industry and the state. I think if the Native gets sufficient pay to save five pounds ($24.30) a year, that sum is quite enough for his requirements and will prevent natives from becoming rich in a short period of time."

"How do you intend to cheapen kaffir (Native) labor?" a Commission member asked.

"By simply telling the boys," replied Albu, "that the wages are reduced."

The infant mortality rate for blacks in South Africa is 50 percent. Of ten thousand blacks who entered kindergarten in 1953, only six graduated from high school.

The National Labor Act of 1953 bars blacks from trade unions and from going on strike. The Industrial Conciliation Act, amended in 1963, says that blacks can never rise above the status of common laborer. The Land Act of 1913 says that no black is allowed "to possess, buy, or sell land in South Africa." The Terrorism Act of 1960 calls for the imprisonment of any black criticizing the government. The Suppression of Communism Act of 1960 carries a five-year prison sentence for any black painting a political poster.

It would take a book to list all the repressive laws in South Africa. The Pass Laws, for example, require blacks to carry one or another of seventeen permits, documents, and passports. The Group Areas Act allows the government to expel black communities from their villages without compensation. The South Africa Act forbids blacks from holding public office. The Separate Representation of Voters Act denies blacks the franchise. The Urban Areas Act brings a ten-year prison sentence to any unemployed black found in a city. The Mixed Marriages Act makes marriages between blacks and whites illegal. The Criminal Law Amendment Act calls for the mandatory whipping of blacks for certain offenses. The Native Labor Relations Act carries prison sentences for blacks absent from work without permission. The Public Safety Law established concentration camps for blacks and permits total press censorship during "states of emergency."

Blacks in South Africa don't have to read law books to know

they are slaves. Trumped-up charges are brought against them so they can be sent to jails which supply *free* convict labor. They pay a far higher percentage of their earnings in taxes than whites do. They comprise a clear majority of the population, yet live on less than 10 percent of the land. Black men are taken from their families for periods as long as five years to work in distant mines. Black women and children live on the brink of starvation while the man is away. The labor service contract a black man signs also applies to any children he has between the ages of ten and eighteen. Any black caught trying to leave the country can be sentenced to death. There is no legal minimum wage for blacks, but there is a legal *maximum* wage. The average monthly pay for black women farm workers is $4.50. Blacks can be arrested for no offense at all. "The legal position today," said Julius Lewin of the University of Witwatersrand, "is such that the police can arrest any African walking down the main streets of Johannesburg (or any other South African city) at any time of the day or night, and any competent prosecutor would have no difficulty whatever in finding some offense with which he could be charged."

South African newspapers carry advertisements for "cookboys," "watchboys," "gardenboys," "farmgirls," and "nursegirls." A black is called "coon," "jigaboo," "nigger," "sammy," or "bushman."

Blacks who are arrested are sworn at, assaulted, shoved, and dragged along. They are not permitted to walk naturally. Black people are humiliated by the police, beaten by them, tortured by them, raped by them, shot by them. On the rare occasions when policemen are brought to trial they are usually acquitted.

Blacks in South Africa are told they are unfit and unclean, yet almost every white home accommodates black domestics. It is unheard of for blacks to dine with whites, yet blacks cook the food, wait on the table, feed and tend the children. There are separate elevators but, if the "Europeans Only" elevator is out of order, whites use the lift reserved for "Non-Europeans." Whites and blacks use different public telephones and rest rooms, go to different theaters, eat at restaurants that are separated by a partition. Buses, schools, and hospitals are segregated and, of course, the facilities for blacks are grossly inferior to those of the whites. Partitions are even erected in factories to separate whites from blacks, although they do the same kind of work.

Black Africans are not the only people ground under by apartheid. There are also the "Coloreds" (people of mixed descent) and the "Indians" (slaves brought from India in 1860 to work the sugar plantations). These people suffer as much as the blacks, but there are not as many of them.

Racism is everywhere in South Africa. A sign above an elevator reads: "THIS LIFT IS FOR EUROPEANS ONLY—SERVICE LIFT IS PROVIDED FOR TRADESMEN, NON-EUROPEANS, PRAMS AND DOGS." Another sign, this one outside a white farm in the Transvaal, says: "DANGER! NATIVES, INDIANS & COLOUREDS—IF YOU ENTER THESE PREMISES AT NIGHT YOU WILL BE LISTED AS MISSING—ARMED GUARDS SHOOT ON SIGHT, SAVAGE DOGS DEVOUR THE CORPSE."

South Africa uses the word "European" inaccurately. In that country it means anyone who is white. It also means some who are not. Because of profitable trade agreements with Japan, South Africa has made the Japanese people "honorary whites."

According to South Africa's own newspapers, more than one thousand blacks are arrested each day for pass violations. In a one-year period, June, 1962, to June, 1963, 82,206 lashings were administered to 17,394 prisoners. In 1966, 65,000 black children starved to death. The life expectancy for blacks is thirty-seven years; for whites it is seventy-two years.

South Africa may be color blind where the Japanese are concerned, but it can tell a black man when it sees one. The great actor, Sidney Poitier, had to indenture himself to producer Zoltan Korda in order to get into South Africa to film *Cry, the Beloved Country*. Tennis star Arthur Ashe was kept out altogether.

But nothing, *nothing* more dramatically illustrates the viciousness of apartheid than the massacre that took place in Sharpeville on March 21, 1960. On that day several thousand blacks gathered outside a police station to protest peacefully against the pass laws. Ambrose Reeves, former Bishop of Johannesburg, described what happened first: "At about 10 A.M. aircraft flew backward and forward, diving down over the crowd, presumably in order to get them to disperse. If this was the intention it did not succeed because the children cheered the planes, and many more people, seeing the aircraft from a distance, were attracted to the police station to see what was happening. I am not aware of the cost to the government of putting a squadron of aircraft into the air, particularly when among those aircraft there were jet fighters. It does seem to me, however, that the aircraft represented a very expensive method of dispersing a crowd which would probably have gone home if a policeman had taken the trouble to ask them to do so."

The protest outside the police station began to take on an almost festive air. People had brought picnic lunches. There was singing. Children played. Then, at 1:30 P.M., the police began to fire into the crowd with machine guns. Immediately the people who had assembled began to run, but the firing continued unabated for a full *two minutes*. Sixty-nine Africans were killed, most of them shot in the back, and 180 were wounded.

Speaking about the Sharpeville Massacre in an address to the British House of Commons, Winston Churchill concluded by saying: "And then was seen what we believe to be the most frightful of all spectacles, the strength of civilization without its mercy."

Bishop Ambrose Reeves conducted his own investigation. Here are his conclusions:

"The truth is that the police at Sharpeville disregarded both the letter and the spirit of their own standing orders and disobeyed the law of the land.

"The officers made no attempt to persuade the crowd by non-violent means to disperse.

"The officers failed to order the crowd to disperse.

"The officers failed to warn the crowd that if they did not disperse force would be used.

"The officers made no attempt to use any form of force less drastic than firearms.

"The officers failed to supervise and control the men under their command.

"The officers took no steps to ensure that if shooting started it would be limited and controlled and could be stopped.

"The constables started shooting without receiving an order to do so.

"Many of the constables shot to kill, not merely to wound.

"They did kill sixty-nine people, including eight women and ten children.

"The shooting was indiscriminate and continued long after the crowd had turned and fled.

"The one hundred and eighty wounded included thirty-one women and nineteen children.

"There was no justification for the police to open fire on the crowd and therefore no justification for the conduct of the police."

What did the government of South Africa do to the policemen who perpetrated the Sharpeville Massacre? Did they lose their jobs? Were they sent to prison? Were they executed? No. Not one policeman even went to jail. Most continued as law enforcement officers. If they issued any expressions of regret, no one heard them. Lieutenant Colonel Pienaar, who was in charge of the police that day, was asked if he had learned any lesson from Sharpeville.

"Well," answered Pienaar, "we may get better equipment."

By refusing to imprison even one of the murderers, the government of South Africa proved that it stands behind its police. Standing behind the government, armed not with a nightstick or a gun but with the power of unlimited money, is your friend at Chase Manhattan Bank—David Rockefeller.

South Africa was in the throes of a dangerous financial crisis in 1961. Worldwide revulsion against the perpetrators of the

Sharpeville Massacre had led to a substantial withdrawal of European capital. Trade unions around the world refused to manufacture goods intended for export to South Africa. Many countries initiated economic boycotts. Churchill of England, Nehru of India, Nkrumah of Ghana—these were but a few of the leaders who scored the South Africa regime and called for an end to apartheid.

But not David. In 1961 he approved a $10,000,000 Chase Manhattan loan to prop up the sagging apartheid economy. Two years later his bank joined with other financial institutions to extend $40,000,000 more in credit. Since 1963, not a year has gone by that the Chase hasn't lent millions to South Africa.

David's loans are not prompted simply by a desire to collect interest. *U.S. News & World Report* (December 18, 1967) provided another reason: "Mineral riches, some known, some merely hoped for, rivet U.S. developers' attention in countries of South Africa. . . . There's a scramble to check out possibilities for oil in the Republic of South Africa's offshore areas. Amoseas, owned jointly by Texaco and Standard Oil of California, is prospecting for oil in the vicinity of Cape Agulhas, Africa's southernmost point. Among others with off-shore-search rights, an affiliate of Standard Oil (New Jersey) is just starting work near the South Africa-South West Africa line."

Mobil, International Harvester, and Chrysler are other companies that David has an interest in that are doing booming businesses in South Africa. Also, Chase Manhattan, besides its own branches, controls the Standard Bank Group which dominates finance in all of Africa.

David visited Africa in 1959. The *New York Herald Tribune* said the tour's aim was threefold:

"1. To open a branch of the Chase Manhattan Bank in the Union of South Africa at Johannesburg, the first in Africa south of the Sahara.

"2. To visit offices of the Rockefeller Brothers Fund, a philanthropic organization of which Mr. Rockefeller is a trustee, in Nigeria and Ghana. Under a program providing $250,000 a year for the next five years, the fund will seek out development projects in small industry and provide technical assistance in cooperation with both local and foreign investors.

"3. To study economic, political and social conditions in Africa in connection with surveys the Council on Foreign Relations is making."

A number of people were not pleased with any of the three purposes of David's trip. Establishing a Chase Manhattan branch in South Africa was hardly the way to show disapproval of apartheid. In addition, much of the money Chase has lent in that country has been used to purchase arms. It is not inconceivable that the guns that killed the Africans at Sharpeville were bought with Chase money. Second, the Rockefeller Brothers Fund is supposed to be a foundation, yet it was scouting out profitable business ventures that the Rockefellers and their friends might want to invest in. Most people have to use their own money to search for new investment enterprises. David uses the tax-free dollars of the Rockefeller Brothers Fund. It costs him not a penny to scour the globe for ways to become richer. Third, studying "economic, political and social conditions in Africa" hardly seems the sort of task a "private" organization should undertake unless, as a number of people say, the Council on Foreign Relations is the "real United States State Department."

When David returned from his African visit in 1959, he said that, while Americans are "instinctively sympathetic" to the independence movement in South Africa, "it is important that we not try to intervene or make inflammatory statements one way or the other . . . people who have tend to confuse rather than help the situation."

It wasn't until 1965, however, that David's position on South Africa became crystal clear. Here is an exchange of letters between Paul Potter, president of Students for a Democratic Society, and Mary W. Schager, one of David's aides at the Chase:

"Dear Mr. Rockefeller:

"The National Council of Students for a Democratic Society has directed me to communicate with you concerning the Chase Manhattan Bank's lending policy in the Republic of South Africa. Our concern grows from our commitment to racial equality and democracy at home and abroad and our knowledge that the policy of the Government of the Republic of South Africa with regard to its black majority is brutal, repressive, degrading, and inimical to the prospects for peace on the African continent.

"It is our firm belief that the United States government and institutions such as yours must cease and desist supporting the Verwoerd regime through trade, investment, and lending. Despite mounting world protest, however, your bank continues to nurture the South African economy. In 1961 your bank made a $10 million in dollars loan to help the South African economy. In 1963 your bank participated in a $40 million revolving credit, replacing an existing credit of the same amount. An institution which shared the interest of mankind in peace and social justice would not aid the South African government in evolving further its policy of apartheid and oppression. Only a withdrawal of support can offer any hope of bringing about a decent and democratic society in South Africa.

"Accordingly, the National Council of Students for a Democratic Society, the legislative body of that organization, demands that the Chase Manhattan Bank cease and desist from lending funds to and in other ways supporting the dictatorship in South Africa."

"Dear Mr. Potter:

"In David Rockefeller's absence from the bank, I am taking the liberty of answering your letter to him.

"We are pleased to learn that such organizations as yours follow banking news, and in particular, our loans to the Republic of South Africa. I understand and concur with your commitment to racial equality and democracy, and hope you will appreciate our stand on this matter.

"If we consider the receiver of a loan to be financially responsible, we do business with him, regardless of his nationality, religion, or political views. A loan to the Republic of South Africa is considered sound banking business, and we feel it would be unwise and unfair if we, as a bank, made judgments that were not based on economics.

"This does not mean, however, that the Chase Manhattan Bank endorses the political decisions of the government of the Republic of South Africa, or any other country which receives a loan from us. On the other hand, we believe it would endanger the free world if every large American bank deprived developing countries of the opportunity for economic growth. If one hopes for changes in the Republic of South Africa, or elsewhere, it would do little good to withdraw economic support.

"We greatly appreciate your thoughtfulness in writing to us on this matter, and hope that this brief outline will clarify our policies."

As radical as it is, Students for a Democratic Society was not alone in criticizing David's contributions to apartheid. At a 1967 stockholders' meeting, Richard K. Taylor, a Chase stockholder from Philadelphia, offered a resolution calling on the bank to withdraw from South Africa. The resolution was ruled "out of order" by chairman of the board George Champion.

Again in 1970, this time with David chairing the stockholders' meeting, a resolution to withdraw from South Africa was rejected. "Such action," said David, "would be most unlikely to change the government's policies and would hurt the country's black population most of all."

David knows better. The plight of blacks in South Africa has worsened since Chase Manhattan went there. Some of the corporations controlled by the Standard Bank Group are not only among the most ruthless exploiters of cheap labor, but of free convict labor.

Nor does the argument advanced by David's aide that banks must make their judgments based solely on economic factors hold water. If that were the case, Hitler's Germany should have received money (and, in fact, it did) from American lenders.

It would take great courage for David to withhold money from South Africa, since certainly there would be other lenders to take his place. In any case, in view of the extreme character of the South African regime, moral pressures may be brought to bear from other quarters to force David to the step he has so far refused to take.

It was a windy day. I had been standing outside the Chase Manhattan Bank Plaza for nearly an hour, the collar of my jacket pulled up against the chill.

The limousine was black and very big. There were four men inside: the driver, two burly types who might have been aides but didn't look it, and David.

One of the burlies opened the door and David stepped out. He glanced into my face but didn't see me. Then he was gone, flanked on each side by a burly, hurrying up steps and through a revolving door, rushing, no doubt, to meetings which would dictate the fabric and quality of my life, of millions of lives.

And he didn't see me.

But I saw him and was frightened.

Chapter XII

➤➤❯❮❮❮

"*D*R. *FRONDIZI* could not have been more friendly," David told the *New York Herald Tribune,* after a 1958 visit with Argentina's president-elect. "He is an alert and intelligent gentleman. We could not have been more impressed."

David remained impressed with Arturo Frondizi for a long time. Few other people did. After only four years of his rule, salaries had risen 400 percent, food prices 750 percent, and other items 800 percent. Meat production dropped from 145,000 metric tons a year to 87,000. Wheat production went down 30 percent in one year. Even electricity became scarce.

"Dr. Frondizi has great prospects of achieving a good government," David said, "not only because of his personal qualities of intelligence and capacity but also because of the popular backing shown by the election results."

John Gerassi, in his best-selling book, *The Great Fear in Latin America,* described what life was like under Arturo Frondizi: "Torture became more common than under Peron; the usual method was the *picana,* a 12,000-volt electrical device that, attached to sexual organs, nipples, or soles of feet, caused unbearable pain (and eventual sterility) without leaving traces. On July 1, 1961, a congressional investigating committee, which had turned up evidence of widespread police torture practices resulting in 38 innocent deaths, was dissolved after a group of policemen fired 200 shots against the Congress building, wounding two bystanders. Policemen were not fired or prosecuted; instead their salaries were raised 35 percent, and on July 25th Frondizi declared a National Police Week."

Frondizi was pro-Nazi. When Adolf Eichmann, who had been kidnaped from Argentina, was standing trial in Jerusalem, Argentina's equivalent of the CIA told the Buenos Aires Jewish community: "There will be a great deal of anti-semitic activity now. We can assure you that no one from your community will suffer, physically or materially, if you cooperate with us. We want the names of every Communist Jew."

Under Frondizi fascism was rampant in Argentina. Stink bombs were thrown into theaters that were showing anti-Nazi films, thugs armed with submachine guns broke into Jewish cultural centers, organized gangs adopted the fascist salute. According to Gerassi, people in Buenos Aires were more afraid of the police than they were of robbers.

In one regard Frondizi's economic policies were a success, and because of that one factor David never said an unkind word about him. John Gerassi explains: "Meanwhile, his [Frondizi's] so-called 'economic program' continued. Mainly limited to giving away oil exploration concessions and boosting production of manufactured goods, this program was quite successful. The once barren deserts in Patagonia, in the South, were transformed into bustling mining centers, with old and new wells gushing out 70 percent of the country's daily needs of 250,000 barrels. (United States oil companies increased their contracts to a value of $1 billion; Standard Oil of New Jersey alone exploited 1,184,000 acres in Patagonia.) Manufactured goods also went up significantly, especially in cars and vehicles."

Frondizi became a rich man while he was in office. And he helped oil companies become even richer. For the common man, however, there was only hunger, jail, or death.

Nonetheless, if David hadn't flattered Frondizi, if he hadn't praised him, if his companies hadn't taken advantage of his corruption, then another David and another Standard Oil would have. David is faced with a dilemma: If he acts according to his conscience, he loses money and maybe even goes bankrupt; if he operates as he has, he incurs the moral indignation of the poor.

Another government that David praised was Colombia's. In 1957, while having the Cruz of Boyaca medal pinned on his chest, he said that Colombia's "democratic traditions are just the same as ours."

Actually, there is little democracy in Colombia. In 1968, the candidacies of two of the four people running for the presidency were declared illegal, and votes for those two were annulled even before the election was held.

At the time David praised Colombia's "democratic traditions," that country's ruler was General Gustavo Rojas Pinilla. Rojas Pinilla had come to power via a military coup, and his four years in office were devoted primarily to enriching himself and his friends.

However, when David supports someone there is usually a reason—an economic reason—and such was the case with Rojas Pinilla. Standard Oil of New Jersey was in Colombia, as were Mobil, Standard of Indiana, and Standard of California. In addition, IBEC manufactured a wide range of metals in Colombia, and also sold chickens, insurance, and mutual funds.

The Rockefeller investments in Latin America are enormous. Standard Oil of New Jersey is in Venezuela, Argentina, Brazil, Chile, Colombia, Ecuador, Paraguay, Uruguay, Nicaragua, El Salvador, and Peru.

Mobil is in Argentina, Barbados, Brazil, Chile, Colombia, Ecuador, Guatemala, Puerto Rico, and Venezuela.

Standard Oil of California is in the Canal Zone, Brazil, Colombia, Peru, Guatemala, Puerto Rico, and Venezuela.

Standard Oil of Indiana is in Colombia, Trinidad, Puerto Rico, and Venezuela.

Of course, the Chase Manhattan Bank is all over Latin America. The countries it does business in have been listed previously. An even more interesting organization, however, is the International Basic Economy Corporation (IBEC).

IBEC was created in 1946, at the same time as the Rockefellers founded the American International Association for Economic Development (AIA). AIA, which was nonprofit, was supposed to parallel IBEC, which was anything but nonprofit. The purpose of IBEC was to set up businesses in poor countries, and AIA was to engage in health, education, and research in those same countries. It soon became crystal clear, even though AIA had been founded amidst a flurry of fanfare, that David and his brothers were more interested in profit than in providing health and educational facilities. In fact, the situation became so lopsided that IBEC (which dealt in housing projects, supermarkets, agricultural processing plants, textile mills, and food-freezing operations) had assets of $142,227,662 at the end of 1965. At the end of 1965 AIA had less than $1,000,000 in assets.

IBEC does business in Venezuela, Peru, Argentina, El Salvador, Colombia, Brazil, Mexico, Chile, Uruguay, and Puerto Rico. According to the April 12, 1968, *New York Post*, the Rockefellers hold 70 percent of IBEC's stock.

Nelson's 1969 welcome to Latin America was much too hot for comfort, and a good deal of the reason that the Latins were hostile was the way IBEC does business. Claiming it was bettering housing conditions, IBEC constructed 14,000 one-family homes in Puerto Rico, but the price of the dwellings ($11,000) was such that only the well-to-do could afford them.

As soon as AIA and IBEC were formed, they began to alienate people. In 1946 AIA conducted a market and product survey of the hybrid seed corn industry in Brazil. AIA discovered that only one domestic company—Agroceres Limitada—produced hybrid seed corn. IBEC then moved in to provide Agroceres with capital to expand. In exchange for the money, IBEC got a piece of the Agroceres' action. Once its foot was in the door, IBEC moved more boldly. Today the company has cornered more than 45 percent of Brazil's hybrid seed corn market, turning what formerly was an indigenously owned business into an American-controlled operation.

IBEC is not popular in Venezuela. As Victor Perlo pointed out in *The Empire of High Finance*, IBEC's dairy company in that country undercut its local competition by mixing imported powdered milk with water and fresh milk. Once IBEC had eliminated its competition, it raised milk prices drastically, charging nearly 50 percent more for milk than was being charged in the United States.

"The Rockefeller International Basic Economy Corporation," said John Gerassi, "has its finger in almost every pie available. And one such pie is INSA, a corporation whose main purpose seems to be to help investors avoid Venezuelan import taxes."

Venezuela has been hit hard by deficits and has been forced to protect its lack of dollars by taxing imports. David and his brothers found a way to beat the Venezuelans out of this tax money. They erected a huge assembly plant, and then outfits like RCA Whirlpool and the Fram Corporation shipped parts to the plant, where finished products were "built in Venezuela by Venezuelans."

Rockefeller-controlled companies extract more oil from Latin America than all other companies combined. And the profits are tremendous. In 1960, Creole Petroleum, the Jersey Standard subsidiary that operates in Venezuela, paid $3.19 in dividends for every dollar it paid in wages and salaries. In 1966, with many of the Venezuelan people hungry, Creole made more than $250,000,000 in profits.

Standard Oil of New Jersey averages about a 7-percent profit on domestic oil operations. In Latin America it averages more than 17 percent. Nor does Jersey worry about taxes. Rare is the year it or any other Standard Oil Company pays over 10 percent in taxes on net profits.

One of the main reasons for the lack of popularity David and his brothers suffer from in Latin America is the fantastic rate at which their companies have been extracting Venezuelan oil. If maintained, many experts believe, all known reserves will be depleted in twelve years.

Profitable as Latin American oil ventures are, however, there are risks, and David may have been seeing the handwriting on the wall when he delivered a speech to the Inter-American Press Association on October 27, 1966, in Lima, Peru. "The private capital which Latin America so badly needs," said David, "will be attracted to the area only if it is given credible guarantees against expropriation and discriminatory treatment as well as credible assurance that equitable repatriation of profits will be possible."

Several years later Peru nationalized a number of Standard Oil properties.

David spends a great deal of time saying how necessary U.S. private investment in Latin America is if standards of living are to be raised. But such is not the case at all. Better conditions for the Latin American people can come only when Latin Americans own their resources. Suppose Venezuela owned General Motors and took all profits back home? Suppose Brazil owned American Telephone & Telegraph? Suppose Argentina owned the DuPont Company?

David Rockefeller and other investors in Latin America are there for one reason: to make money, the more the better. Adolph Berle, an adviser to President Kennedy, said that "preachments about the value of private enterprise and investment and the usefulness of foreign capital (in underdeveloped countries) were a little silly. Foreign and/or private investment may industrialize, may even increase production, and still leave the masses in as bad a shape as ever."

Latin America has had no significant economic growth in the last fifteen years. "Of 200 million Latin Americans," Gilbert Fuentes wrote in *Monthly Review,* "140 million suffer from endemic diseases, 70 million are outside the monetary economy, 100 million remain illiterate."

The United States Agency for International Development, supposedly formed to help Latin American countries, has another purpose: According to *U.S. News & World Report,* January 24, 1966, AID uses taxpayers' money to insure large corporations against losses from inconvertible currency, revolution, war, and nationalism.

While David and other investors enjoy the good life, Latin America goes deeper into debt. Sanz de Santamaria, chairman of the Inter-American Committee of the Alliance for Progress, was quoted in *Economic Affairs*, June 1, 1966, as saying: "Latin America's debt amortization alone will require $1.7 billion this year (1966), thus pre-empting 16% of all export earnings."

David wants to make profits without taking a risk. In 1968 he suggested that Congress pass a bill providing a 30-percent tax credit in the first year on private U.S. investments in developing countries. "It is also my conviction," said David, "that by broadening still further the risk guarantees that our government provides for qualified overseas investments, more businesses would avail themselves of venturesome opportunities."

Latin America is larger and potentially much richer than the United States, yet the yearly per capita income is less than two hundred and fifty dollars, and in places like Paraguay, where Jersey Standard is searching for oil and where Nelson Rockefeller embraced the dictator Stroessner, the per capita yearly income is around sixty dollars.

David pretends to believe that the term "exploitation" is a Communist-inspired slur on good business practices. Nonetheless, it is true that he has made enormous profits in other countries without significantly bettering the people's standard of living. In fact, David would not have invested abroad at all if there hadn't been the prospects of large profits and inexpensive labor. The very reasons he invests in overseas enterprises help guarantee that living standards will remain low.

David is no better and no worse than many other businessmen. He is only bigger—so big that no corner of the world is beyond his reach. His life style has such monarchial trappings that Alexander, once conqueror of the known world, would weep with envy.

David's kingdom has no borders. And so long as people are born, so long as they strive for profits, so long as they abdicate the power that is rightly theirs, the kingdom will grow and live, stretching into infinity.

Born rich, he has grown richer still. Born to power, he understands its many uses and employs them to the full. His name is David, one of the true inheritors of heaven's graces. Yet perhaps he should consider what Shakespeare wrote about another king:

> *Expose thyself to feel what wretches feel,*
> *That thou mayest shake the superflux to them*
> *And show the heavens more just . . .*
> *So distribution should undo excess*
> *And each man have enough.*